Enabling End-Users

CHANDOS
INFORMATION PROFESSIONAL SERIES

Series Editor: Ruth Rikowski
(email: rikowski@tiscali.co.uk)

Chandos' new series of books are aimed at the busy information professional. They have been specially commissioned to provide the reader with an authoritative view of current thinking. They are designed to provide easy-to-read and (most importantly) practical coverage of topics that are of interest to librarians and other information professionals. If you would like a full listing of current and forthcoming titles, please visit our web site **www.chandospublishing.com** or contact Hannah Grace-Williams on email info@chandospublishing.com or telephone number +44 (0) 1865 884447.

New authors: we are always pleased to receive ideas for new titles; if you would like to write a book for Chandos, please contact Dr Glyn Jones on email gjones@chandospublishing.com or telephone number +44 (0) 1865 884447.

Bulk orders: some organisations buy a number of copies of our books. If you are interested in doing this, we would be pleased to discuss a discount. Please contact Hannah Grace-Williams on email info@chandospublishing.com or telephone number +44 (0) 1865 884447.

Enabling End-Users

Information skills training

ANN POYNER

Chandos Publishing
Oxford · England

Chandos Publishing (Oxford) Limited
Chandos House
5 & 6 Steadys Lane
Stanton Harcourt
Oxford OX29 5RL
UK
Tel: +44 (0) 1865 884447 Fax: +44 (0) 1865 884448
Email: info@chandospublishing.com
www.chandospublishing.com

First published in Great Britain in 2005

ISBN:
1 84334 108 5 (paperback)
1 84334 109 3 (hardback)

© A. Poyner, 2005

Cover images courtesy of Bytec Solutions Ltd (*www.bytecweb.com*) and David Hibberd (*DAHibberd@aol.com*).

Printed in the UK and USA.

Contents

Introduction

End-user information skills training can be fun. It can be rewarding. It is now becoming an essential tool in the educational role expected of library and information professionals. It can also be daunting. Many such professionals may be unwilling converts to this extension of their job description and need help. Others will be taking up designated skills training posts but lack experience in getting started. It can be regarded as a positive evolution from a more traditional professional role with opportunities to broaden career horizons.

As part of the preparation to devise information skills training programmes, it may be useful to review existing library and information services together with end-user perceptions of these services. A fuller understanding of end-user needs will make it possible for librarians and information professionals to adopt effective training and learner support roles.

Brief information about user surveys and end-user training needs assessments is given to enable information professionals to formulate survey ideas. These can then be used to contribute to discussions within library teams about how these tools might be implemented in service development.

This book aims to assist information professionals who are planning to offer end-user education and information skills training through personal tuition. It does not cover the development of computer-based training packages or distance learning programmes.

Many general principles apply across information skills training and the development of searching techniques. These mainly relate to the exploitation of databases and electronic resources. They may be referred to in more than one chapter of the book or suggested linked chapter reading may be indicated.

It is hoped that the simple steps outlined can assist library and information professionals enhance information literacy among their end-users. The ideas and suggestions are based on the personal experience of the author.

About the author

Ann Poyner is a professional librarian and has worked in the (national) health service, managing library and information services and establishing library IT infrastructures, specialising in literature searching, giving end-user education on information retrieval techniques and accessing electronic information resources. As a member of an outreach skills trainer group she contributed to pioneering the delivery of information skills training in non-library environments in the workplace and clinical setting.

Recent work emphasis has been on training and development with contributions to specialist training and knowledge projects sponsored by the London Deanery (London Department of Postgraduate Medical and Dental Education – University of London). This work was presented as a paper at the European Association for Health Information and Libraries (EAHIL) in Sardinia in 2001 and has been published in the *Health Information and Libraries Journal* (2002), vol. 19, no. 2, pp. 84–9, with a second article in the *Health Information and Libraries Journal* (2004), vol. 21, no. 1, pp. 57–60, describing a subsequent workshop training programme.

The author now works as a freelance information skills trainer living in north Essex, and is Chairman of a local Patient and Public Involvement Forum (PPIF) representing healthcare views of the local community.

The author may be contacted via the publishers.

Seeking information

Chapter contents

This chapter provides coverage of:

- involving the end-user;
- threats to library and information services;
- promotional activity;
- library location;
- library environment;
- library guidance.

Transition from passive to involved end-user

The traditional pattern of libraries being a repository of books, journals and related materials where library staff answer the questions posed by readers or users is changing. Certainly queries are still answered and information provided. However, library users are now less passive in their behaviour and increasingly wish to be involved in the information retrieval process. Frequently information sourcing is electronic. Outside the immediate library environs people will explore the Internet looking for information, often without the necessary searching skills. Library and information professionals are tasked with enabling their end-users to fully exploit all aspects of the library service available to them plus tutoring them in information skills to empower their use of a variety of information sources.

Before planning information skills training activity it is beneficial to stand back and review your library and information service. Think about its place within your organisation and how it functions.

Countering threats to library and information services through promotion

The provision of a library and information service within an organisation may be questioned. The costs and space required in the 'information age' will be closely examined. Increasingly individuals are expected or are being encouraged to seek information for themselves.

If the quality gateway provided by the library is threatened, how can information professionals ensure that their skills remain relevant to the information seek, search and retrieve cycle?

Promotional activities include the following:

- raising the library profile within your organisation;
- marketing your library and information service: giving workplace demonstrations of available information resources or making a presentation at staff meetings within your organisation;

- identifying key individuals within your organisation to act as library and information service champions and asking such individuals to become members of any library committee or information service group that exists. This will give them direct access to influence decision-making;

- understanding any differing information needs various staff groups have within your organisation;

- targeting departments within your organisation and tailoring services to meet their information needs;

- becoming involved in any educational programmes within your organisation: induction days, audit activity or staff development.

Through this promotional process you will better understand the needs and expectations of the staff you serve. It will be easier to present what is available and what is possible, and argue the case for change or extra funding.

- It is important to be seen as a professional, offering unique skills to the organisation.

- Explore opportunities to become a member of key organisational committees, working parties or management boards. This will inform you and enable you to reach a wider audience of people.

- The library location may not be central – find ways of ensuring that it is not forgotten.

- Try to anticipate trends and plan accordingly.

- Share experiences with colleagues throughout the organisation.

Well-briefed library staff can respond to changing demands from users.

- Users will ask for help to search for information. Be well prepared to give it.

- Library staff may be required to offer detailed and specific help to end-users to enable them to successfully search for information themselves. This mirrors the humanitarian aid concept: while a bucket of water will help an individual today, helping them to dig a well will help them for a lifetime.

Information seeking and provision are part of a life-long learning continuum. The library should be seen as a key player in this process. With the growth of information technology within organisations there may be pressure to absorb library and information service points into broader information departments. It is important to ringfence essential elements from libraries and play a leading role in shaping change.

Computer networking within organisations makes an increasing range of information sources available to individuals at their place of work on their desktop – often many of these derive from traditional library funding. Make sure that the library service is identified with such resources and make clear the added value the library can offer in their use. Try and contribute to organisational decision-making about information provision and demonstrate convincingly how information professionals can positively assist the organisation.

Library location and environment

The library location

Make sure everyone in your organisation can answer the question, 'where is the library?' Unless potential end-users know you exist, you will not be able to enable them in any way! Approach your library as if a stranger to the building in which it is located. Think about the following points.

- Are there any signposts indicating its existence or location?

- Are such signposts consistently placed to lead to the library?

- Are members of the reception staff in your organisation aware that there is a library? Ask a colleague to telephone your organisation and request the library or you by name. The response may be revealing.

- Can you place library details on noticeboards throughout the organisation to advertise the existence of a library? Make sure that such notices are well designed with a clear layout and that they are consistent in style and clarity.

- If the organisation is spread across several sites, have all the necessary library details and signposting been replicated on each site?

The library environment

Once end-users have found you, is your library welcoming and easy to use? This may be relatively straightforward if you only have a small collection of material. However, if you have specialist services or facilities these may not be so obvious to end-users. If end-users ask for help you will be able to explain everything to them but you may be busy doing other things or your end-users may have an independent nature and wish to explore resources for themselves. Approach your library as if for the first time and honestly test whether everything you know to be available is clearly highlighted to end-users.

If your information service relies heavily on the telephone or postal delivery check these aspects out from the user perspective.

It is easy to live within the limitations of your library and become so familiar with the layout that you cease to question 'how things are'. Not everyone has the opportunity and pleasure of planning a brand new library or the requirement to reorganise existing facilities. However, to help deliver service objectives, undertake a theoretical planning exercise in which you give very careful consideration to the relationships between the presentation and location of stock and services.

- Where are staff work positions or offices located?

- Can they observe the arrival of library users – is there more than one entrance?

- Can staff respond quickly to end-user enquiries?

- Do end-users have to enter library office space to interact with staff?

- What security implications are there if staff leave their office area to answer enquiries? This can be an issue with single or small staff teams.

- What stock is used most frequently? Often it is the current journal issues. Make sure that these are located close to the library entrance for quick and easy browsing, avoiding transit through the library and possible disturbance of those studying.

- Are popular reference works prominently displayed? Can staff supervise them?

- If computers and Internet access are available, can this aspect of the library service be supervised adequately? End-users will often require help and staff need to be on call to answer questions, demonstrate how equipment works, troubleshoot when problems occur and supply more paper for the printer.

- Can library users understand the order in which the book stock has been arranged? Great care may be taken in book selection, classification and processing but unless end-users can quickly understand the logic of a classification scheme and locate stock on the shelves with the help of clear signage, the stock may be under-exploited.

- Is there a library catalogue that is accessible and easy to understand for end-users? Where is it positioned? Is it computerised? Are there clear instructions about how to search the catalogue?

- Are the arrangements for collecting materials ordered by end-users on inter-library loan or requested as photo-copies clear and unambiguous?

- Do you a have a photocopier? Where is it? Can you supervise its use?

By addressing some of these issues, it may be possible to make slight modifications to your library layout and design a more logical environment for your end-users. At least you should be more aware of the difficulties your end-users may face when entering the library that is 'home' for you but may be strange territory for them.

Details of staff and their contact information should be immediately on view. Opening times should be clear. Any out-of-hours access arrangements should also be clearly stated with key or swipe card entitlement outlined.

Try to produce a layout plan on a large scale and place it in a prominent position. Ensure that all library stationery is always available and instructions about how to fill it in and where to leave it for processing are clearly displayed. If you have archive material in alternative storage areas, ensure that such stock is advertised. Study areas away from the workplaces of end-users can be seen as a valuable asset. The library can be regarded as a haven. Try to create such a space where possible. Make any policy about food or drink in the library quite plain and apply it fairly.

Library guidance

Decide carefully what library guides and forms you think are necessary. Design them simply with the end-user in mind. Detail all aspects of the library and information service and describe what, where and how. If you expect end-users to fill in forms requesting information or for a literature search to be done on their behalf, give them a reasonable framework in which to express all aspects of their enquiry. This will save wasted time and effort on your part. Any request forms for inter-library loans or photocopies should prompt end-users for every piece of information that will identify the exact item required. Design all forms to a standard, using the same font, any library or organisational logos and a similar question sequence. Develop a library and information service 'brand'.

In some situations you may have a relatively small library with responsibility for offering an information service to a membership at a regional or national level. Telephone and postal responses in these circumstances will dominate your work with occasional visits from members. Ensure that all the aspects that apply to using a library are translated into how you respond to and communicate with your library and information users at a distance. Prepare an information pack that can be sent to new members with all the details about the types of service available and how to request help, with full staff contact data. Use request slips, as would be used by an end-user in the library, and complete them during the telephone call so that all requests are expressed in the same format for processing. Design compliment slips and standard covering letters to send out with requested information or loan items. Additional blank forms can be sent out at the same time for future postal use. Keep detailed records of your activity for reference in case of a query or lost items. Use e-mail communication to keep in touch with library and information service users – perhaps publish a regular e-newsletter to update users and remind them about all aspects of your service. Set up routine request forms online with opportunities to request information or renew loaned items.

Once you have improved, where possible, the library experience for your end-users or perhaps contributed to any reorganisational activity related to the library and information service, you could contemplate your end-users' perceptions of the services you offer.

Identifying key issues

Chapter contents

This chapter provides coverage of:

- end-user awareness and perceptions;
- survey ideas and methods;
- information audits;
- mind mapping;
- interviewing techniques;
- responding to survey results;
- identifying training needs;
- assessing training needs;
- pre-training self-assessment.

Finding out about end-user awareness and perceptions of library and information services

Be alert to end-user comments and suggestions. If questions are frequently asked about particular issues or topics, ask yourself if you are making appropriate information resources available. If it becomes clear that library users are struggling to use your services or find information, ask yourself why. Be observant and listen to what is being said either directly to you or within the library.

You might like to explore end-user awareness or needs and library usage more fully by carrying out a library survey. This can be time consuming and requires careful planning. It can take several forms.

Survey ideas and methods

- *Examine your membership records.* How thorough are you in keeping them up to date? Do end-users have to show a membership card to use the library and information service? Do you have different groups of members, i.e. students on placement within your organisation, who may qualify for temporary or limited membership? You can then use an analysis of this data to accurately note the active library membership within your organisation as a percentage of potential membership numbers. This will highlight those people who do benefit from using the library. It may also enable you to identify departments or groups of staff who do not feature in your membership spread. Try and find out why this is so and how you might be able to target them with details of relevant information resources.

- A *simple e-mail communication.* Contact everyone in your organisation to advertise a specific service or library event – the message could include a few simple questions about library usage that people might be prepared to answer. Just to know that they have opened your e-mail might be helpful (how many people in your organisation might be deleting messages from the library unread?). If you plan to use e-mail as a method for a more in-depth survey of library use, it might be advisable to send an alerting message first, so that people are prepared to receive a fuller communication.

- *An end-user survey or an information audit.* Think carefully before embarking upon a detailed survey. It takes time and planning. Be sure that you can respond to any findings. If you raise expectations among your end-users and potential users and then appear not to change what you offer or do, they may be disappointed. The exercise could be detrimental. When was a library survey last conducted? If people are troubled too often, they may not willingly engage again and your results may be unrepresentative or the response rate poor. What do you really want to find out? If you cannot definitively answer this question yourself, then think again before you trouble your end-users.

Mind mapping

Before carrying out a modest information audit of your library and information service, spend some time carefully thinking about all aspects of your service. It may be useful to consider creating a mind map to assist you in the grouping and summarising of your ideas.

Mind maps allow you to structure your ideas and show the relative importance of different aspects of the service areas under consideration. The visual format allows freethinking across the topics represented. Work quickly to jot down all the aspects of the service you wish to examine. Try and work with colleagues, both from the library and information team and from end-users who are willing to contribute to the process.

The example of a mind map shown in Figure 2.1 was produced by Aileen Wood, a Training and Development Facilitator, as part of an information audit carried out by voluntary library staff of the Millie Hare Library at St Helena's Hospice in Colchester, Essex.

- Write down the key subject at the centre of the page.

- Draw lines out from this to major subject subheadings.

- Indicate any subsidiary level of information related to the subject subheadings by another line.

- Radiate out further lines with notes as required.

- Show any major links between subject subheading sets.

Survey questionnaire

The information recorded in this way (or by simply listing and grouping topics in a more traditional way) can then be used to help you draft an information audit questionnaire or user survey questionnaire. An example of an information audit questionnaire is given in Appendix 1 – this audit was carried out at a hospice where the ratio of paid staff to volunteer staff was 150/800. A 10–15 per cent sample was identified for interview.

Topics that can be covered by an information audit questionnaire will be related to your own particular library and information service. The selection may cover the following.

Section 1: General awareness of library services

Use this section to seek information about end-users' or potential users' awareness of:

Figure 2.1 An example of a mind map

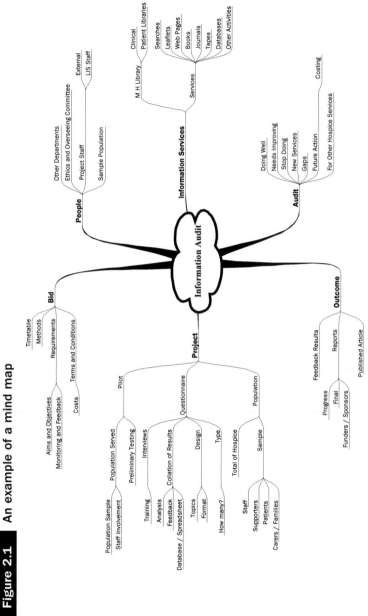

- the existence of a library within the organisation. If yes:
- ask about the frequency of use;
- ask about knowledge of library opening times;
- ask about preferred opening days and times;
- ask if they had been given an induction to the library services;
- ask whether specific aspects of the service have been explained.

A negative response to the first question could be followed up by asking the end-user: 'Having been made aware of a library – would you use it?'

Section 2: Staffing

This section can be used to ask about:

- how helpful end-users found the staff to be;
- how satisfied they have been with the information given;
- whether staff have been available when required.

Section 3: Services and systems

This section can list all the services offered by the library. Ask end-users to indicate:

- awareness; and
- use.

Also use this section to ask about:

- use of the library space – computer rooms or study areas or reading rooms;

- use of resources by format, e.g. book, journal or video, and indicate on a scale of frequency of use, such as 'never', 'sometimes', 'frequently' or 'all the time';
- opinions about book loan periods;
- opinions about any library fines policy (state the current fine rates and their basis, i.e. linked to associated university policy);
- opinions about the currency of library book stock in both loan and reference collections;
- location where service is used, if available on multiple sites.

Journal subscriptions

An important and expensive element of library and information service provision is the journal stock. Ask end-users:

- to list up to five journals that they consult on a regular basis;
- to indicate their awareness of access to e-journals;
- to state their use of e-journals.

Inter-library loans

Ask questions about their use of this service or their opinions about any charges made for it or their willingness to pay within listed cost bands.

Photocopying

State the current charges made and ask about their willingness to pay within other listed cost bands.

Other specialist services

Seek information about their awareness and use of any special collections or services you offer in the library.

Specific databases, CDs, videos or the Internet

Structure questions about any of these items, asking again about awareness and use.

Website

If your organisation has a website you can ask about end-user awareness and use of that site, and in particular about the library and information service pages.

Subject coverage

It can be useful to give end-users an opportunity to comment on the subject coverage of your library and make suggestions about areas they consider to be inadequate. Ask for details.

Section 4: Other comments

Record any other observations, ideas or comments. A limited use of 'open questions' can offer interviewees an opportunity to express concerns or detail experiences in a way that helps you adapt and develop your services.

Action to implement a survey

Once you have drafted your information audit questionnaire or user survey questionnaire, take time to think about it carefully. Ask colleagues for their comments and observations and encourage them to share any experiences they have about drafting and using such questionnaires.

Review your organisation and user membership to determine a suitable representative sample of people to contact about completing a questionnaire. Involve management, departmental heads and other lead staff for their cooperation and support. They may wish to nominate staff from their department or section to become involved in the audit or survey. In a smaller organisation you may aim to contact a larger number of people or try to talk to most library users and potential users.

Try, if possible, to interview those taking part and complete the questionnaire as part of that interview process. This should ensure a comprehensive response. If a mailing of questionnaires by post is undertaken, take time to chase and follow up replies. If your survey or audit is substantially carried out by personal interview, it would useful to indicate (perhaps with an asterisk) those questionnaires completed by individuals on their own. It may useful to be aware of this when analysing the results.

Seek approval of the finalised questionnaire from any relevant management-level, board, ethics committee or other overseeing authority within your organisation or institution.

Ensure that any senior management giving their support and backing to the audit or survey are consulted about any issues they wish to be covered in the audit or survey. Include questions to elicit information about these issues so that a response can be given. For example, if there is a contract between your parent organisation and an external body to deliver specialist or specific library and information services to a particular group of users, e.g. students on placement, then it may be important to monitor use, perception and quality issues with these users.

When drafting questions that require a qualitative assessment response try to give four answer categories, e.g. Very Good – Good – Satisfactory – Poor. If you give five answer categories there is a tendency for interviewees to opt for the middle measure and this dilutes the response – specificity is lost.

Process

Once a questionnaire is agreed, it is useful to carry out interviews with a pilot group of end-users. Identify a small number of people that you think will be willing to help with the information audit or survey and ask them to come to the library to be interviewed. The group could meet together for a briefing about the aims and objectives of the information audit and then be interviewed individually. This could be concluded quite promptly if two or three members of staff are engaged in the exercise. If you undertake this on an individual basis, then you could arrange to meet with the pilot group members either at their workplace or in the library by appointment but try to conclude the interviews on the same day or within a few days.

The testing of the questionnaire in this way will help to identify any weaknesses or lack of clarity about the questions posed. It may become clear that a particular question is not making sense to the interviewees. Revise the questionnaire as required.

Produce a cover sheet identifying the details of the interviewees and attach this to the questionnaire at the point of interviewing. A database or master list can be produced listing the interviewees with this full information until the interviewing phase of the survey or audit is complete. This will help you check against your list of potential interviewees and keep a balance between the various staff groups being targeted. Each questionnaire should be given a unique number. This enables everything to be checked during the audit or survey period to guard against approaching the same person twice or double counting results. When the interviewing stage is complete remove the identifying cover sheet to ensure anonymity when examining the data later. However, you will still have a record of the staff group and other data against the uniquely numbered completed questionnaire. This will allow you to analyse the replies in greater depth. Instead of just being able to quote that a percentage of people replied in particular way, it will be possible to break down that reply by staff grade or group, male or female, work location or full-time/part-time, and so on. Such data may be relevant to understanding a particular response or to explain a response. At this stage, however, delete the names of interviewees from your database or master list so that no one response can be traced back to an individual.

Interviewing

Not everyone has relevant interviewing experience or skills. However, you can prepare yourself to undertake this process. Give consideration to the following:

■ Maintain impartiality – this is very important. You have to remain dispassionate when asking questions and not react to any comments that are made about the library and information service. For example, someone may say that they are totally unaware of the library opening hours and that they have not seen a notice about them. You know that such information is prominently displayed.

You must not intervene and make defensive statements about the matter.

- Be consistent in your presentation of the questions – if a question relates to knowledge about a range of resources it may be better to prepare a 'flash card' or information sheet with brief summary details. This allows for the interviewees to read the information for themselves rather than you laboriously explaining everything to everyone with the risk of sounding weary or missing something out.

- Avoid bias – do not give help or clarify a question so that a more desirable answer is obtained.

- Be confident when reading the questions – try not to stumble over your words.

- Give thinking time to the interviewees when longer questions are being asked.

Give your interviewees the option of having the questionnaire sent to them in advance so that they can think about their responses before the structured interviews take place.

Analysis

Think about how you intend to record the results. If you have spreadsheet or statistical software, mirror the questions in this software. It will make data entry and later statistical analysis easy. If the number of interviews being conducted is relatively small or you have no experience of using spreadsheet software, a simple five-bar gate recording of the findings can be made and calculator-assisted totals established. You can print out a copy of the questionnaire with increased spacing between the questions to allow you to mark it up in this way. The pattern of responses will hopefully show the interaction between issues being questioned. If there is a negative response to a particular topic, it should be possible to discover from supplementary questions why end-users had a problem with that aspect of the service.

Outcomes

Present findings of the information audit or survey clearly. The spreadsheet totals version can be accompanied by a written report that states the aims and objectives of the audit or survey with a commentary on the results. A summary of responses to any 'open' questions can be included.

Response

You may include in the audit report a section on the response of your library and information service to the findings. Identify all positive aspects of the findings. Examine carefully any critical responses and try to understand why the end-users found difficulty in using your service or were disappointed in the service they received. Highlight issues that could be addressed with additional resources.

Service planning

Using a considered assessment of the information audit or survey findings, incorporate the ideas and issues arising from the exercise into your future work and service planning. It will be possible to make the case for increased resources or the introduction of an enhanced service based on 'hard' evidence. Even if you are not immediately able to make changes indicated by the information audit or survey results, at least you are better informed and will be able to counter adverse comment by being aware of it, or offer explanations to end-users about the limitations of your current service range.

Random survey

As an alternative to a detailed survey it is possible to obtain a quick snapshot of end-user awareness or response to your library and information service by carrying out a random survey within the library. If you have devised a full information audit or user survey questionnaire, this could be used in full but it would probably be better to edit it down into a simple key-point questionnaire outline.

Decide on a timescale, perhaps one or two weeks depending the amount of staff time you feel you can devote to the exercise, and break each day down into time slots. These could be half an hour after the library has opened for two hours, two hours over the lunchtime and then mid-afternoon for two hours. You may also be aware of a particular pattern of usage that you wish to tap into and plan your time slots accordingly.

Within each time slot try to approach a set number of library users, say three or four, and ask them if they would be willing to spend a short period of time answering some questions about their experience of using the library and related information services. Explain briefly the purpose of the survey, whether it be to monitor library use by different staff groups, explore stock usage, investigate end-user training needs, identify gaps within the service, or whatever it is you are surveying at that time. Some people will not be able to cooperate due to work pressures or indeed not be willing to help you but usually a sufficient number of end-users will respond, especially if the process is simple and does not take up too much time. You can try to ask a varying cross section of end-users but the sample will not be scientifically drawn.

This immediate and personal interviewing can reveal quite a range of information that can then inform your service planning. Make sure that you have clear notices up in the library to give advance warning of the survey period with an explanation of what you are trying to achieve. Note in the report of the findings if you think that the pattern of library usage in person was different, i.e. possibly less during the survey period – perhaps a reaction to the survey being conducted. Some of the data you collect during such a survey can be measured and quantified against specific questions but much of the data will be qualitative. Giving end-users an opportunity to talk freely may yield views and ideas that need to be noted in detail for analysis later.

Doing a spot check of end-users in this way can provide useful information without embarking upon a full-scale information audit or survey. One member of the library staff can be assigned to carry out the work or perhaps a small team could share the work. A student taking a library and information degree or qualification may agree to undertake the survey as part of their studies.

Identifying training issues

If questions are asked about awareness of data resources and end-user ability to exploit them, you will then have very useful information that will enable you to identify key training issues and decide about how best to address them. Once you are sure what your priorities should be, you can initiate or extend existing training sessions.

If end-user requirements indicate a major increase in training time, you will have to draw up a training programme to reflect these user needs. It may be possible to accommodate additional training sessions within existing staff limitations by rearranging tasks. The audit or survey findings may show that a significant investment is required to fully respond to end-user training needs. Use this information to formulate a training strategy within the library and information service and negotiate with the management of your organisation to try and ensure that end-user needs are satisfied.

If you work as part of a wider network, opportunities may arise for training activity to be planned on a broader basis with specialist training shared between libraries. Many library and information professionals do not benefit from such arrangements and have to include all training activity within their own working week. It is then important to offer information skills training as part of a realistic work programme.

Do a small amount of training well rather than trying to cover all topics on demand. Build on this work and continue to make the case for additional time and resources to expand the training work. Hopefully this will be forthcoming if it is an organisational priority.

Key training issues

Information about end-user training needs may be available to you from a recent information audit or survey. Alternatively you could carry out a specific training needs assessment. This could take the form of a very extensive survey across all staff when you are in a position to really respond to the demands that will be forthcoming. It is more likely that you will initially raise awareness of existing skills training opportunities that you offer. These should be based on the databases and other resources available in the library or via library networks. Identify key resources or newly introduced resources that end-users should be familiar with and confident to use.

Decide how best to break down the training components into manageable training sessions that will allow your end-users to attend. Depending on the organisation in which you work, staff or students may be allowed specific study time or designated library time – this will enable you to plan quite detailed sequential training sessions. However, end-users are often trying to fit in the improvement of their information skills by attending training sessions during their lunch breaks or you may be asked to make such training available before or after work times.

You will have to develop a mixed training portfolio to encompass a progressive approach to some topics covered by more than one training session, with other rather intensive and comprehensive 'catch-all' sessions for those end-users who feel that they can only attend one training session at random intervals. The comprehensive training session can be rather overwhelming for end-users. You know all the aspects of searching techniques or subject coverage in relation to particular information resources and you want to tell your end-users about them, and indeed they would benefit from knowing them all. However, there is a danger of information overload in these circumstances. Try and balance the giving of essential information with some additional information in summary format, perhaps supported by training notes, examples and exercises. Encourage them to come back for more!

Assessing training needs

Use ideas that you have had in relation to a fuller information audit or survey and draft a short questionnaire covering the resources you have available to your end-users to determine end-user awareness and use plus their training requirements.

- List all the information resources available in or via the library and ask end-users to show whether they are aware of them.

- Ask end-users to indicate which resources they would like help with.

- Allow the end-users to indicate the level of training required, i.e. introductory, intermediate or more advanced. This will involve an element of self-assessment. The description 'advanced' may deter some end-users. Try different ways of describing the training level, such as 'more detailed' or 'part two' or 'follow-on'.

- Try to establish their availability to attend training sessions by asking about days of the week and specific time slots.

- Explore end-user preferences about attending training in the library or at alternative venues.

- Ask about computer skills. Check on the need for help with computer use and basic software understanding.

- Allow an open question for end-users to express an interest in training being provided on resources not listed.

Pre-training self-assessment

It is useful to ask end-users attending your training sessions to complete a pre-training self-assessment form. This is not always feasible. You may offer 'drop-in' training sessions on an informal basis. At these sessions you will have to quickly assess the competencies of the individual or group and direct your training accordingly. A booked training session or course allows you to try and gather information about those taking part in advance. It does help you devise training and exercises at an appropriate level but always be prepared to adapt your training session in response to what happens on the day. Flexibility allows you to give the best training to any particular group.

Self-assessment relies on an individual recognising his or her own needs and skills. They may under or overestimate their talents. They may not understand fully what you are asking; for example, if you ask about Boolean operators they may hesitate when in fact they have been using AND, OR and NOT in their searching without knowing the 'jargon' involved. Just to clarify some of these issues can be helpful and dispel uncertainty.

Keep the assessment questions simple. You can ask the end-users to complete a post-training assessment form based on the same questions. This at least measures their perception of their own change or improvement (if any). It can be a quick and ready way of noting progress.

Examples of a pre-assessment questionnaire and a post-training evaluation questionnaire are given in Appendix 2.

Participants who lack computer skills may slow down your information skills training sessions. If this happens frequently, you may have to state that pre-training computer literacy is required. Enlist the help of colleagues within your organisation to deliver general computer or IT skills training. It may be that your IT department already offers an internal training programme working towards a recognised qualification, e.g. the ECDL (European Computer Driving Licence). Make sure that your end-users are aware of these opportunities. Publicise them at any library and information induction session, linking them to the pursuance of information skills training. This will enable end-users to fully exploit all the information resources available.

3

The information professional as educator

Chapter contents

This chapter provides coverage of:

- the changing role of the information professional;
- the librarian as educator or trainer;
- the examination of personal strengths;
- communication in user education;
- interpersonal skills;
- the training experience;
- forms of communication;
- the evaluation of training – questions to ask.

The changing role of the information professional

It is worth reflecting on the traditional role of a librarian or information professional. From an appreciation of existing strengths it is possible to consider future service delivery. Much is made of the transition to the use of electronic resources but how do these relate to traditional library provision?

Historically librarians were responsible for the collection and preservation of books. Their role grew into that of professionals who acquired, organised and developed that print-based collection and then started to include stock in varying formats like audio, video, microfilm, multimedia or computer programs. They disseminate information to end-users and improve access to information often beyond the physical limits of their library. Wide ranges of library and information services are now made available via electronic networks.

With pressure upon space within organisations, it is sometimes assumed that digital or electronic resources can replace what is currently offered. It has to be appreciated that less space does not necessarily represent cost savings. Electronic information requires a high investment in equipment and if new services are to be sustainable there are annual revenue and budgetary implications. Electronic journal subscription costs can escalate quite rapidly.

It is true that many people do search for information and access resources away from the traditional library. Book and journal collections that have been skilfully acquired and maintained over many years represent a rich source of information that should not be lost to end-users. As a library or information professional you can aim to develop a hybrid service harnessing the values of both dimensions. The structure of information in a virtual library environment presents problems of organisation and classification.

A key area of change is the introduction of electronic journals. People welcome the idea of immediate desktop access to journal articles without time spent visiting the library, carrying out a literature search to identify relevant articles and then waiting while their request is satisfied either by a photocopy of a stock item or one obtained from another library. There is a danger with desktop e-journal access that other journal sources not available through that given system can be ignored and overlooked. What may seem a simple service to the end-user actually requires detailed negotiation and organisation on the part of the librarian or information professional to make electronic journals available to their users. There can be problems when activating electronic versions of journals subscribed to in hard copy. Publishers often set up their systems to recognise the IP address of a particular computer but when computers in the library or on the individual desktop sit behind firewall security measures they cannot be recognised. Often the electronic subscriptions have a short archive or do not offer access to very recent issues depending on access conditions. Collective subscription agreements can make economic sense to groups of libraries operating within the same sector.

However, electronic subscriptions only allow access to the journals and at the end of the subscription period the libraries do not own the journals and have no collection for reference. People do still like to hold and handle the real thing. Browsing through a journal issue encourages lateral thinking and exposes the reader to a broader range of literature. It can sometimes be more relaxing than staring at a computer screen.

The Internet presents new information horizons to end-users. Librarians must be on hand to help their end-users, many of whom are inexperienced Internet searchers, to exploit the potential of the Internet and retrieve relevant information. You may find yourself acting in an informal mentoring role as you guide your end-users to extend their knowledge base.

The librarian as educator or trainer

The virtual library world requires the librarian or informational professional to take on an educational role. It is becoming more important to define and develop this aspect of the role. Occasional help and guidance within the library is one level of assistance but to fully equip your end-users to search for, retrieve and evaluate information, you will need to examine your own skills set.

The disciplined approach to collection management, information retrieval and dissemination that is inherent in librarianship offers an opportunity to respond to the changing patterns of information needs and resources with some precision.

Personal strengths

Examine your own strengths. Are you better suited to a backroom role, ensuring that the library and information collection is selected, processed and maintained to a high standard? This is important work and feeds directly into the quality of the service and how end-users can be served, drawing on an excellent and up-to-date collection of materials. Do you enjoy interacting with end-users and perhaps adopting an outreach role – taking the library service out to end-users at their place of work or study? Are you a good negotiator? This is an essential talent when bidding for funding, space or service recognition. Can you think strategically? Delivering a good service now is important operationally but an ability to plan ahead and anticipate the range of resources becoming available and matching them to end-user requirements within a realistic financial framework ensures that your library service evolves with your organisation or institution. Do you have computer literacy skills? The roles of librarian and computer expert are increasingly becoming blurred. You may have to assist end-users with basic computer skills before they can advance to information retrieval skills. Are you able to assume the role of educator or trainer? It is vital that all resources accessible in or via the library are promoted and that end-users are enabled to fully understand their significance and acquire the skills to exploit them.

Information skills training work has become an integral part of the expanding role of library and information professionals. Often this aspect of library and information work is being grafted onto existing job descriptions and individuals in post may not always feel comfortable or confident about taking on the task. They may be interested in developing the role but feel under tight time pressures. New posts are being created to deliver information skills training with the person appointed joining the existing library team. In some situations it will fall to just one or two individuals to respond to the wide range of professional activity expected of them. End-user expectations are rising all the time – in part fuelled by the high-quality library services available to them.

Many library and information professionals who become involved in information skills training decide to undertake some form of educational or teacher training to facilitate their work. This dual ability can contribute to the overall educational role of their organisation. This is clear in an academic environment but other organisations that are responsible for education and the continuing professional development of their staff could benefit from the more comprehensive qualifications of their library staff.

Library trainers often enhance their own skills by sharing experiences with colleagues working in similar situations.

They might form specialist professional groups within their subject sector that meet regularly to exchange views, ideas and training materials. This work can inform the setting of training objectives and the preparation of coursework. Sharing expertise in this way can bring about consistency in training standards. It also prevents time being wasted duplicating effort in isolation.

To offer information skills training sessions within your library you will need subject competence, confidence and a desire to help end-users through a personal interface. You must want to convey your knowledge to other people. Are you able to engage with others, make them feel relaxed and willing to learn? Handouts and library guides give your end-users information whereas good information skills training offers them understanding.

Communication and interpersonal skills

Communication involves sending or receiving information. As an information professional delivering information skills training you have to be a good communicator. Having an in-depth knowledge about a subject or data source is not enough: you have to get your message across to your end-users.

The first step is defining your message. Once you have decided upon a programme of information skills training sessions, study days or workshops, you must set about drafting their content. Have clear and achievable objectives about each session or module and articulate all the elements to be included against each topic or information source. Design a logical sequence of information that flows through the training session.

Prepare well and try to relax. Practise in advance and time the presentation carefully. This will avoid a rushed performance. Ask a colleague to listen and comment. Pace your presentation, breathe slowly and deeply, and try to demonstrate calmness even if you feel a little nervous. If you do stumble over words or miss something out, do not apologise as this may give a negative feel to the session. Just take another deep breath and with an explanation or review of the subject continue with the training. Do not over-complicate what you say. You may have 50 interesting things to say about a topic but it may be more valuable to communicate 15 key points really clearly in a relaxed style rather than go into information overload and overwhelm your group. Does your voice carry well in the training venue? Test yourself. Know your topic well. This will allow you to answer questions clearly and with confidence. If you are asked a question that you cannot answer be honest about it, find the information later and communicate the answer to the participant concerned.

The training experience

Allow time at the beginning of any training event for participants to settle down and get comfortable. Start with an informal introduction about yourself and state clearly the outline for the session, the training objectives and the expected learning outcomes. This can be a very straight-forward process if you are offering one-to-one tuition but it is still important not to rush into 'doing something'. Allow the end-user(s) time to think their way into the training experience. Remember that you know in detail what you are about to embark upon but to your end-user(s) it will be a revealing process. Group introductions work for small groups but will not be possible for much larger groups where you are not offering limited individual attention but rather giving a lecture or presentation.

Remember you are leading the individual or group. Be approachable and flexible but keep to your targets as far as possible. Make eye contact with participants that you are speaking to and listen attentively to what they are saying or asking. Do not be embarrassed by silence – use it to consider a response or allow the group to take a mental break. Some aspects of information skills training involve direct information delivery and resource demonstration. End-users will require help and explanation to fully discover all aspects of the searching software associated with different databases. Even intuitive searching will not necessarily reveal all the details. Opportunities early in the training session for participants to express their understanding about information resources and information retrieval can be a helpful collective communication exercise. This improved awareness within the group can assist later in small-group work or shared use of computers.

Forms of communication

Communication can take various forms. Primarily we think of the spoken word but visual communication can be powerful – colourful pictures, graphs or diagrams can convey a message or fact quickly. Some people find it much easier to understand numerical data in this format. Variety reduces boredom. Think about expressive facial communication that instantly shows how somebody is feeling or thinking. Observe your group. Beware of giving away your own feelings at difficult times.

Always produce information that is easy to understand and follow. Use a variety of mediums – PowerPoint or other presentations, overhead projector slides, large-screen Internet projection, flip charts to record group ideas and handouts to remind participants of all the key topics being covered. Make it clear at the beginning of a training session that you have handouts available. This will save participants scribbling notes throughout the session and perhaps missing some of the important concepts. You may decide to distribute handouts at the beginning of a session for participants to follow as you go along or you may think that having the notes in front of them will be a distraction and so make them available later instead.

End-users need to feel at ease and ready to learn. You hope that they are attending your training sessions because they want to but in some cases their line manager, departmental head or tutor may have sent them. It is important for you to recognise any resistance in the group and overcome it if possible. Unwillingness to concentrate on the part of some participants may unsettle the group. As the trainer you need to control events but not dominate them. Try varying the pace of your delivery and give opportunities for topics to be talked through again if it is apparent that participants are struggling to understand what you are saying or if it is clear that they are becoming tired.

An important part of the learning process is hands-on experience. It can be useful to prepare set exercises to be done during or at the end of a training session. Hopefully this direct application of what you having been talking about will truly assist the participants in their understanding of the information resources under review. It will build their confidence. Facilitate this activity and be on hand to answer queries and help the participants solve the set questions. While it is a test, it is not intended to become an agony for the participants.

Evaluation

Evaluation of information skills training can be regarded as a form of two-way communication. It can help you assess library performance, redesign training materials and make you think about training methods. It can also demonstrate whether or not your end-users are making the best use of the available resources. Honest comment about a training experience can inform your future planning of training events. There is a dilemma about creating a time at the end of the programme for evaluation forms to be filled in or whether to give them out for returning later. On the day, people may wish to leave promptly and therefore fill in evaluation forms in an ill-considered rush; on the other hand, if left to complete them later, they may forget altogether or their memory may fade about certain aspects of the training session. If specific funding has been allocated to the training event and the sponsors require a value assessment from the participants, perhaps to decide about follow-on support, then it will be a priority to carry out a good evaluation on the day of the training event.

Questions to ask

Here are some suggestions about the range of questions that you could ask as part of a training evaluation:

- How had the participants heard about the training event? This will test your marketing activity.

- Ask for opinions about the training programme, with a possible breakdown by each session if it is a longer course, in terms of:

  - ability level;

  - relevance to their interests and expectations;

  - quality, style and knowledge of the trainers.

- Ask about the reason for attending the training session.

- Explore any barriers or problems faced in accessing the training.

- Ask about the suitability of the length of the training session(s).

- Ask for comments on the venue and catering. This will be important if you are using a venue for the first time and wish to consider its future use.

If an evaluation form is sent out to participants after a training event to collect data over a period of time when training is being offered, it is then possible to explore:

- confidence levels of participants – has there been any improvement?

- any opinions or preferences about where the training was delivered – e.g. in the workplace or IT department training facility or library;

- any problems about putting their newly acquired skills into practice – e.g. time pressures, access to an Internet connection and computer or difficulties in constructing a search strategy;

- willingness to pay for the training they have received – availability of training budgets or personal contributions. This information can help you decide about increasing the range of training on offer if additional financial resources can be identified.

4

The searching process and searching techniques

Chapter contents

This chapter provides coverage of:

- searching techniques;
- constructing search strategies;
- framing the question;
- questions to ask before searching;
- database characteristics;
- combining searches;
- Boolean operators;
- limiting searches;
- quality filters;
- managing search results;
- critical appraisal and bias;
- evaluation of results.

Introduction

The number of sources of information is increasingly rapidly, and there has been an explosion in Internet sources. It is important for you to explore all relevant resources available in the subject area you work in and present them clearly to your end-users. Medicine and healthcare are particularly well served with a comprehensive range of information sources and many subject-specific databases and authoritative sources accessible via the Internet. Other disciplines do not enjoy such a long-standing structured literature. Academic institutions face the task of covering a wide range of subjects and ensuring equity in provision.

Hierarchical sources of information

The idea of thinking about information sources based on their significance can help end-users to consider the relative value of the information they find. Help end-users to identify quality material by thinking about reviews or specific authenticated studies. Encourage them to look for evidence. Opinion or advice given by a recognised expert in the field or the knowledge of a senior colleague should nonetheless be critically examined.

Constructing search strategies

It can be a highly valuable exercise to prepare a presentation or lecture exploring various aspects of searching techniques. It will enable you to fully think through all the useful ideas about searching for information. You may be asked to make such a presentation to groups of staff at induction events or as part of audit activity or at an event outside your workplace. There may not be time to cover all the topics in your talk but having an extended text allows you to be in a position to use key parts in response to enquiries. The remainder of the chapter gives a suggested presentation outline for adaptation. It specifically relates in detail to database searching but the concepts are valuable in broader searching activity.

Searching techniques

To search: 'try to find something by looking carefully and thoroughly' (*Pocket Oxford Dictionary*, 9th edition, 2002)

There is a tendency now for end-users to rush into looking for information without taking care to note what they have done or where they have searched. This often results in them having to repeat some searches to ensure that they really have covered a particular resource, database or website.

Outline some of the key sources available to end-users. It can be interesting to ask them about their most frequently used sources and why they find them helpful. Consider:

- books and journals;
- databases;
- the Internet;
- expert opinion;
- experience.

Increasingly library users think of asking for a computer search or use their own computers as a first resort in seeking information. However, other information sources can still be of value and are often easier to access for some end-users. Users often express their interest in books and journals.

They may be more familiar with these information sources. Suggest alternative sources that will complement their existing information-seeking patterns and build on their experience.

Framing the question to ask – getting started

- Search terms
- Search strategy
- Searching interface

Before end-users start to search they should have considered carefully what information they are seeking. Encourage them to think about all the search terms they want to use. Ask them to start to construct a search strategy using those terms. Make sure that they are familiar with the searching interface of the data source before they start. Considered preparation will result in better outcomes.

STAC – a search strategy framework

- *Stop* and consider carefully what information is required.
- *Think* about all the concepts, terms and synonyms.
- *Analyse* the ways in which the search can be combined or limited.
- *Construct* the best search strategy possible.

This simple framework encourages end-users to remember the key components to consider when starting out on a searching process. Not all the elements may be relevant to every enquiry but it is useful for people to be aware of the searching stages.

Often end-users think of a very broad subject term and may be unaware that they can be quite specific about stating exactly what they are interested in. Help them to tease out all the aspects of a given topic so that their search will yield relevant material. You can give end-users a simple example of the subject specification trail. If they said they were interested in, say, fruit and searched using that term, it would result in many hits. They may then intend to scan through the results to pick out what they are specifically interested in – this would be time-consuming. Their interest may in fact be apples rather than fruit in general – better then to search using the term apples or do they really mean apples and pears? Perhaps on closer examination they really want information on varieties of apples or when to prune apple trees. They may be aware of a recent article or report on the subject that they want to track down and therefore will not be looking for references dating back many years. Show them that they can fully state their information needs and build up a search strategy covering all the aspects that are vital to their search. By searching on all the aspects of the search topic that they can identify and then combining or limiting them logically they will arrive at a manageable set of references to finally scan and select from.

Questions to ask before starting a search

Why do I need this information?

Is it a passing interest of no lasting consequence or is it related to serious study or research or about an active work situation? This will determine the time spent on the search and the depth of searching required.

What am I going to do with this information?

If the information is to be applied in a work or research situation, it is important for end-users to understand and be able to explain clearly exactly what they have done to find the information. They need to be able to evaluate the source and accuracy of the information to be used. This is especially relevant if the information is to be acted upon in relation to health or legal or business matters for example. Will the implementation of the information impact upon other people? If the information is used to support study or education the reliability of the source must carry authority.

When do I need this information?

It is of no value undertaking an extensive search, locating references not immediately available in the library, if the information is required to support an imminent presentation or meeting. It must be realised that a quick search is not necessarily a very thorough search.

Is there a particular population group involved?

If a disease is being researched in relation to a particular age group or legislation about a specific group, such detail must be included in the search strategy. Without such detail a large number of references may result from a search that on scanning do not necessarily indicate their precise content.

Time will be wasted checking through the search results and end-users will become frustrated and express lack of confidence in the databases or other resources being searched.

Is there a particular treatment or intervention or interaction to be explored?

It may be this precise aspect that is important to the end-user. Ensure that they have fully expressed every element of their search interest.

Is a particular time period relevant?

Data sources have varying archive material. Many end-users become familiar with one or two databases or resources that they use regularly and make assumptions about other information sources based on this experience. This may result in disappointment if a particular time-span is vital to their search and a resource being searched does not cover that period. Point out these issues to end-users.

All these questions should become second nature to anyone undertaking serious searching and hopefully become instinctive when planning a literature search.

What makes database searching different

The reasons for this may be summarised as follows:

- the structured nature of databases;
- the use of index terms;
- the facility to explode or focus;

- stated inclusion criteria;

- consistency of the presentation of results.

It is important for people to be aware of the nature of the information source they are using. Databases are structured in a formal way and if you understand the way in which information has been entered into a database, it is easier to 'interrogate' that database.

People sometimes use the terms keyword or index or free text. Help them understand what these mean in the context of any database they are searching.

Sometimes within the searching software there may be an opportunity to explode (expand) the range of terms being searched or focus (make more specific) a search term. Be sure that end-users can decide when to use either of these features if they are available. Prepare some examples of searches to demonstrate the alternative results obtained.

A database will have stated inclusion criteria that make it easier to know the range of information covered, as opposed to a general information source when it will not be clear what has been included or excluded.

The search results from a database search are presented in a consistent manner which makes them easier to scan and select relevant items.

Database content and selection

This may be considered from the following perspectives:

- type of material and references;

- size;

- time-span.

Not all information sources or databases contain the same type of material. Many will contain only journal articles but some may include book chapters or reports or websites. It is important to know the nature of what you are searching before you begin or you may waste time looking in an information source for a particular item not covered by that source.

Information sources vary in size. Results will be different depending on whether it is a long established database with millions of records (e.g. Medline)[1] or a recently started database with records amounting to only a few hundreds in the first few years. Ensure end-users think about this before they begin searching. Linked to this is the time-span covered by a data source.

Database selection

The database to be selected may:

- be bibliographic;
- provide systematic reviews;
- be subject-specific.

Information professionals can easily fall into the trap of using their own jargon without explaining to their end-users exactly what is meant. Try to explain the difference between a bibliographic source and a general information source. It is important to clarify the nature of high-quality information sources like systematic reviews. This information is relied upon heavily in the healthcare sector. Highlight the existence of any subject-specific databases related to the work interests of your end-users. This will allow them to focus on relevant material.

Getting to know about databases

In order to get to know a database, users should:

- explore the 'help' button;
- ensure they understand any 'quirks' in the searching software, e.g. use of upper or lower case, quotation marks or brackets.

If an end-user is faced with a data source and no personal help is available encourage them to use the help button or help screen where available. Make sure that you have used such built-in help yourself so that you are confident that it really does help! Print out any of the help sheets and add them to your own portfolio of training notes.

It is especially important to emphasis any quirks a database may have in how the searching software has been written. Many of these are not obvious to the end-user and while information about them may be buried in the help screens, often there is no mention of them on the initial search screen. An example of this problem is the question of using upper or lower case. Increasingly, software is not case sensitive but in some databases it is important to use Boolean operators in upper case e.g. PubMed – a free access version of Medline. It is common now to use inverted commas when searching the Internet to ensure that linked words are searched as a phrase – equally this may be useful in some database searching. The use of brackets can clarify the search sequence. Most searching software acts upon searching instructions from left to right.

Searching specific fields may require a specific way of entering the search. If any data sources you use regularly have a particular way of entering author or journal title requests make sure your end-users know what to do. Some databases have a dedicated author or journal search screen where help is usually given.

All these issues, once mastered, will ensure that more accurate and relevant results are obtained. Sadly not all searching software is designed to correct searching errors at the point of them happening. If end-users are unaware of this they may be puzzled at the results they get. Tell your end-users to remember issues such as single or plural terms, or differences between English and American spelling. Equally, if very few references are found on a topic that should yield a greater number advise your end-users to check their typing skills – a mis-spelt word may be the problem. It is interesting to note that some original spelling errors get through the editing process and can be found!

Text words and index terms

- Text word searching looks for the occurrence of a word or string of characters in the text.
- Index terms are the controlled vocabulary applied by indexers in the construction of the database.

Explain these differences to users as required.

Combining searches – Boolean operators

Once all the search terms have been explored it is useful for end-users to be confident about combining terms to narrow their search down to a manageable number of records to scan and select. Not everyone has heard of Boolean operators or Boolean logic and many are reluctant to admit that they are not too sure about how to apply AND/OR/NOT. It is well worth fully clarifying these concepts to users because if they are misapplied poor search outcomes will result:

- *AND* focuses a search – both/all search terms must be present in the final set of references;

- *OR* is more – any of the search terms must be present;

- *NOT* excludes an unwanted concept.

AND seems such an expansive word that many people expect to get a greater number of hits when using it but make it clear that AND focuses or narrows the search. OR means more and will result in more records being found. Advise that the use of NOT may result in loosing some relevant records in the overlap. Figure 4.1 illustrates the Boolean operators further.

Truncation and wildcards

- Search looks for the stem of the word using either * or $ signs.

- Check the symbol used in a particular database:

    Example: Cyst* = Cyst, Cysts, Cystic, Cystitis, etc.

Truncation is another of the searching aspects that can confuse end-users. It can be overused and result in massive combinations of shortened terms that make the searching software struggle! Likewise, clarify any implications of the use of truncation such as changing the operation of the searching software. Sometimes an algorithm behind the

Figure 4.1 The Boolean operators

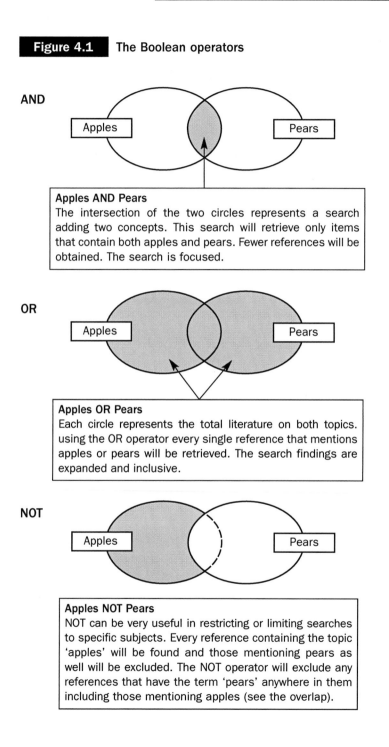

AND

Apples | Pears

Apples AND Pears
The intersection of the two circles represents a search adding two concepts. This search will retrieve only items that contain both apples and pears. Fewer references will be obtained. The search is focused.

OR

Apples | Pears

Apples OR Pears
Each circle represents the total literature on both topics. using the OR operator every single reference that mentions apples or pears will be retrieved. The search findings are expanded and inclusive.

NOT

Apples | Pears

Apples NOT Pears
NOT can be very useful in restricting or limiting searches to specific subjects. Every reference containing the topic 'apples' will be found and those mentioning pears as well will be excluded. The NOT operator will exclude any references that have the term 'pears' anywhere in them including those mentioning apples (see the overlap).

scenes in the searching software carries out a complex searching sequence that may be 'turned off' when truncation is applied.

Limiting searches

Explore the opportunities to limit or refine your search by:

- publication date;
- publication type;
- age group;
- subset;
- human/animal;
- gender.

This is a good way of refining a set of search results to produce a set a records as relevant as possible. Not everyone is aware of the variety of ways in which a search can be limited. Highlight the various options available in each database or information source.

Quality filters

In some databases there may be opportunities to apply special mini search strategies, often called 'quality filters', to tease out very specific aspects of a search topic. A key example of these can be found in medicine to identify particular aspects about a topic such as aetiology, diagnosis, prognosis or therapeutic interventions.

Check out any such filters in databases that you use and make such possibilities known to your users. Think about appropriate examples in the subject area in which you work. They can be helpful in assessing the quality and reliability of search results.

Suggest to your end-users that they create and save a mini concept search to be run together with any new subject search to filter out the required aspects of special interest to them. This will save them time entering the regular search term each time and aid current awareness.

Managing search results

This involves:

- printing;
- saving (search history, results) to disk;
- sending (e-mailing results, current awareness services).

Having carefully coached your end-users in good searching practice, it is then important to enable them to print, save or send their results with confidence. Make sure suitable information about such matters is displayed and make it clear whether or not downloading is allowed or if any conditions apply within the library environment.

It can be helpful to give brief statistical information about the key databases or information sources you have available in the library. End-users can then have a better under-standing of such resources. For example:

- *periodicals (in a given subject area)* – quote the number published worldwide and the percentage not referenced in major databases;

- *websites in Europe/worldwide* – if data is available try to indicate the number covering your subject area and the rate of growth.

Database details and access

Ensure that your end-users are aware of how to request or register to obtain any necessary passwords to gain access to the resources available to them.

A brief outline of each database available assists understanding. Give information about:

- the publisher;
- how many versions there are and how they are accessible;
- searching software used;
- how many journals are indexed to create the database;
- the spread of journal publication, i.e. American bias, European coverage;
- how many records are contained in the database;
- how many years the database covers;
- any specific index or thesaurus terms used in the construction of the database.

Just as information professionals devise detailed information skills training opportunities for end-users, software producers are becoming aware of the reluctance of many of those end-users to fully learn and exploit the sophisticated searching software associated with many databases. Alternative searching modes are being developed that will allow free text questions to be asked as a way of interrogating databases. Software is being designed to interpret the searcher's request. However, all the searching theory that can be conveyed to end-users will hopefully enable them to appreciate the complexities of the databases they are using and value any process that makes it easier for them to search for information.

Try to be enthusiastic and encouraging when engaging with your end-users. Smile, even when talking on the telephone – it will show in your voice!

Critical appraisal and bias

End-users should develop skills to allow them to evaluate and judge the material they find when searching. If their work is research based it will be important to conduct an exhaustive search and select high-quality references. The principles of critical appraisal skills extensively employed by healthcare practitioners to implement evidence-based practice may help your users critically assess the information they find. You may be able to facilitate the teaching of critical appraisal skills for groups within your organisation using in-house expertise or by inviting an outside speaker to talk to staff or run a workshop.

Critical appraisal

Critical appraisal is a technique associated with evidence-based medicine. However, the general principles it espouses of identifying the strengths and weaknesses of pieces of information, often research based, can be applied more extensively. When evaluating an information source or document encourage your end-users to consider the validity of the information and how it was collected plus its relevance to their specific needs.

Bias

Ask your end-users to think about any bias in their search results. It can occur at any stage of a study from its design to the application of the information arising from the study or research. Sometimes studies with negative or statistically insignificant results are not put forward for publication and any review of the subject they cover may be incomplete as a result. There can be selection bias when study subjects are chosen in a way that can increase or decrease the strength of the apparent outcomes. The key question to address is whether or not the results of a study may have been unduly influenced by bias. This would make any conclusions drawn questionable. Observational study designs are more susceptible to bias than experimental study designs.

Evaluation by information type

Print resources

There are some general criteria that can be applied to any print information source you are using:

- *Author* – who is the author? Is it clear? What are their credentials? Have you heard of them? What else have they written?
- *Date* – check the date of publication and any references quoted (are they up to date?).
- *Publisher* – does the publisher have a good reputation for quality material?

- *Journal* – type (commercial, academic or research based)? Has the article been peer-reviewed?

Internet resources

Remember that the Internet is not generally quality-controlled, although individual sites may offer good editorial control and well stated quality criteria – check carefully. There are many websites suggesting criteria to think about when evaluating Internet resources. Try searching for a selection of these, especially any that relate to your subject area, and then compare the advice given. In assessing the quality of the information found, here are a few points to consider:

- Who has provided the information?

- Are author contact details available?

- Check the domain of the document and which institution publishes the it. *Note*: .ac (academic), .gov (government), .org (organisation), .co/.com (commercial).

- How objective is the web page? Is there a commercial message?

- Is the information backed up by evidence?

- Is the site clearly laid out with easy-to-follow links?

- Is there a date when the site was last updated?

- Are any links given? Are they also up to date?

- Can you verify the information given in other information sources?

- Are there clear instructions about using the site?

- Are there keyword searching or Boolean capabilities?

It can be helpful to include a summary of the key evaluation points you consider most important in any searching skills training notes you make available to your end-users. It is important that they are aware of evaluation and quality issues as they search for, find and select information.

Note

1. A bibliographical database containing over 12 million records produced by the National Library of Medicine (NLM) in the USA.

5

Preparing training materials

Chapter contents

This chapter provides coverage of:

- library guides and handouts;
- resource-specific instruction;
- devising exercise and question sheets;
- questions to explore electronic resources.

Library guidance

Always pay attention to the quality of any library guidance or handouts that you produce as outlined in Chapter 1. This will be the first experience of your service for your end-users. Make everything clear, concise and accessible. This is a starting point in the process of empowering your end-users. Enable them to full appreciate and exploit the resources available in your library and then help them to look beyond the library environment to embark upon their own information-seeking and research.

Changes in technology are facilitating the expansion of the traditional information professional's role into one of educator and well as provider. When training sessions or courses are being offered it is very important to prepare carefully and produce suitable training materials in support of your work.

Preparing instruction leaflets and resource-specific materials

Take care and time to prepare any training material. Review all existing training notes or guidance. Increasingly, you will be giving help with the exploitation of electronic information resources. Remember that end-users will require help to interpret and evaluate these information resources – see Chapter 8.

When reviewing existing training notes consider the following:

- How long have the notes been in use?
- Do they fully reflect all recent changes to the databases or information sources they relate to?
- Are they easy to read?
- Are they readily available in the library?
- Are they used?

It is easy, when familiar with an information source, to overlook essential steps in the process of searching it well. A step-by-step approach to drafting training notes or teaching materials will result in a practical and useful end product.

- Carefully and methodically work through a searching process for a given database or information source. Write down every step in detail.

- Remember simple instructions like 'switch the computer on' or 'left/right click' the mouse or 'highlight' as required. It is very easy to assume that an end-user will think of all these general points for themselves and it may be that such an apparently obvious process is missed.

- Try to think of every variable or choice at every stage of the process.

- When you think you have completed the draft, sit down and work through the instructions you have written down. You will probably find that some aspects of the process have been overlooked or not explained fully enough.

- Correct the draft.

- Then ask someone to act as an end-user guinea pig to pilot the instructions and comment on their helpfulness.

- Use any feedback to refine and edit the draft before putting it into use.

- It may be useful to add some background explanations about aspects or coverage of a particular database to assist in its correct use.

- Also prepare a short reference sheet based on the longer instruction leaflet. This can act as a quick reminder to an end-user who has not used that database for some time or as a speedy outline for those in a hurry.

Many shy end-users will appreciate a detailed guide to enable them to work through a searching process quietly on their own. If problems arise they will be better able to articulate the question they want answered based on what they have done so far.

- Try to develop a 'house style' for any of the leaflets you produce so that they are easily recognisable and identified with the library and information service.

- Remember to revise them at regular intervals and repeat the validation process.

- Ensure that any changes to the searching software or presentation of search results are immediately incorporated into any instruction leaflet on offer. Failure to do this will dent the confidence of end-users in your assistance and this may be difficult to regain.

It can be frustrating when searching software changes significantly or perhaps a national subscription agreement for a particular government or research sector is renegotiated and a different supplier is used. Any new or revised software has implications for retraining work and the revision of related training notes and exercises.

Non-library skills

It may also be useful to have simple guides available in the library to help your end-users improve their knowledge of Microsoft Windows or other operating systems in use as well as of word processing and presentational software packages. These skills make searching electronic information resources much easier.

Exercise and question worksheets

With any skills training session it is very useful to have a variety of exercise sheets for participants to work through as part of the training programme. An open time slot for participants to explore information resources for themselves can also be an interesting way to build confidence and experience. However, if you rely solely on an unstructured searching period it may not achieve the desired outcome. Participants may be getting tired and therefore not be able to concentrate on the searching process carefully, or happily depart from the training topic and search for personal information instead. If computers are shared between two or three participants, one of them may dominate the searching process and the others lose out on gaining experience. There is nothing quite like doing it for yourself to check out your understanding of what you have been taught.

- Try to draft about ten to twelve questions on an A4 sheet.

- Make any questions you set varied and interesting.

- Allow the questions to be tackled in any order.

- Allow adequate time for the participants to get into a searching mood and adapt to the task they have been set.

- Aim to include questions that make the participants look at and search specific aspects of a database or use a specific Internet site.

- State that they should answer a particular question using a particular database or website.

Ease and speed of searching are important factors in encouraging end-users to seek information. Therefore do not make the questions too obscure. If you are working with the same group over several training sessions you have the opportunity to increase the degree of difficulty in the questions you set.

If you are training a subject-related group of staff within your organisation or a grade-related group, ensure that the questions you set reflect their specific work interests and level of knowledge. It can be of help to them to draw up a matrix listing several websites related to their work and get them to fill in comments across the form recording their views on speed of search, ease of use, relevance of material, indication of latest update, new websites of interest found through links and whether they would use that website again. The group can share their assessments during a brief group discussion at the end of the searching session.

This feedback comment on Internet searching and opinions about website use may inform you about your own library or organisation's website design and improvement.

Setting questions to explore electronic resources

- Start from an information topic your users should be aware of and work back to setting a question that logically leads them to the web page on which you found that information. It is always amusing to observe what participants actually do and how they find the same answer!

- Ask a question that demonstrates either the limitation of a website or the searching sequence required to unlock information. For example, ask if a particular academic library has a book on a given subject by a specific author. This will highlight the process of first locating that academic institution and then finding the link to library services and then checking out the accessibility of the library catalogue before being allowed to interrogate the catalogue itself.

- Ask a question that should logically be answered by searching a key government or official website and encourage your end-users to look at that website first. This will alert them to the range of information provided by that website for future reference. It may also demonstrate how easy or difficult it is to search that particular website. Show the end-user group you are training how to get the best out of any website that should play an important part in their future searching activity, especially if it is one that is not particularly user friendly. Sometimes there may be a valuable archive resource tucked away that may be lost to the more casual Internet user.

- Ask participants to look for information on a specific topic on three different websites (either of your choosing or leaving them free to identify likely websites themselves) and then suggest that they compare the information found – is it similar, more or less detailed, equally up to date and easy to validate?

- Ask a question that causes the participants to seek out key charities or organisations linked to specific subjects.

- Ask a question that allows participants to explore a website linked to their professional body. This may show them how to find information about examinations, qualifications and board or committee membership relating to their continuing education and development.

- Ask participants to search a subject of their choosing and comment on the number of key websites identified in the results and which ones they would use again.

- Ask some questions not related to work topics and encourage participants to explore resources for finding out about, say, people, maps or transport issues in their own locality. This is a refreshing change of emphasis.

Try to vary the range of websites you expect participants to look at and the likely time required to get at the information you intend them to find. Allow for some light relief among the questions.

Always double check the questions the night before a training session and ensure that the sequences and links you found when setting the questions are still valid. End-users will remember problems and apparent blunders. Be able to demonstrate the searching sequence you had in mind and explain why some websites are important and should be looked at regularly. This can be done as a collective shared activity at the end of the session or you can make yourself available to the participants during the exercise session by offering individual help to group members.

Try to build in some 'letting off steam' time and vary the pace of the training sessions. Some end-users will welcome additional question sheets to work on away from the formal training programme. It is useful then to make it clear that you are available to answer queries and give follow-up help.

6

One-to-one tuition

Chapter contents

This chapter provides coverage of:

- ad hoc training;
- one-to-one individual tuition;
- careful preparation;
- the independent end-user;
- external training opportunities;
- communication skills;
- telephone contact.

Ad hoc training

Any response to an enquiry that involves some sort of teaching explanation can be classed as one-to-one tuition. Such interactions happen all the time and can be time-consuming. It is useful to prepare a response to requests for help in searching or using a database or information source. Draft an instruction leaflet or leaflets that can be used as an introduction to any particular topic. The logical sequence of information in such a leaflet can become second nature to you in giving help to end-users and ensure that there is some consistency in your response. You can learn to 'plug into' the sequence at different points depending on the nature of the request for help and the ability level of the enquirer. Often requests for help come in pressured time slots and it may only be possible to give essential pointers which in themselves may help the immediate information enquiry but which will not enable the end-user to manage the search process fully for themselves in the future.

It is at this point that you can give the leaflet or other prepared tuition notes to the individual user and encourage them to use them, perhaps with further personal assistance, on another occasion. Make sure that such written, CD or networked help is always available close to the information source or computer workstation to which it relates.

Plan to offer one-to-one tuition on a formal basis at an agreed time and location with clearly specified parameters about what topics and help will be covered. This can be in response to a request for help or training slots can be advertised within the library on an appointment basis. A full programme of end-user training can be developed across a variety of subjects and a detailed portfolio of instruction leaflets can gradually be built up.

It is not necessarily cost-effective to offer individual teaching sessions and such tuition may be restricted to those unable to attend mainstream teaching sessions. However, if the ability levels of participants in small-group work are too variable it may be advisable to revert to one-to-one tuition. Alternatively, you could structure your training sessions with a general opening demonstration of key points, followed by longer hands-on work during which time you give targeted help to each participant. Presentations and demonstrations of databases or information sources can be successfully delivered to small and medium-sized groups. The size of the group may depend on the number of workstations or computers available if the teaching involves hands-on work by the learning group. Theoretical talks can encompass much larger groups.

One-to-one tuition can also take the form of offering mediated searching help. As you work closely with your end-user you can gently introduce an educational element.

Individual tuition by appointment

Giving individual tuition can be challenging. Not everyone feels comfortable working in such an intimate setting. Remember you are the information specialist and your end-users are there because they want to learn.

However, one-to-one teaching can be a valuable learning experience for the end-user. It can also inform you and help you revise existing teaching programmes by giving you specific insight into aspects of the information needs of the organisation. Senior staff may be unwilling to join multi-disciplinary and multi-graded teaching sessions. They may be wary of revealing their lack of knowledge. Equally some members of staff may find it difficult to be available at regular teaching session times or request help at their place of work within the organisation.

Use any personal teaching opportunity to enhance the reputation of the library and information service and emphasise the value of information.

Being well prepared

- Review your general teaching materials in the light of the role and work of the individual learner.

- Draft a brief introduction to the concepts you are trying to convey. As you talk through these concepts it allows a short 'breathing space' to the individual end-user to adjust from their busy work schedule into a more receptive learning mode.

- Try to establish in advance their level of knowledge and competence.

- Give worked examples to illustrate key features in an information source that reflects the subject interest of the individual.

- Devise any questions or exercises based on the identified subject area of interest to the individual to encourage exploration of the information sources being demonstrated.

Be prepared for the unexpected

Individual learners are just that and they will probably act in an individual manner. Quite senior staff may at first be unsure about their relationship to you and how much they should allow you to do the talking and be a passive learner at first. At some stage and often quite quickly their status gives them the confidence to intervene in the learning process and you have to be ready and able to run with their agenda and respond to their questions. They may wish to show you a favourite information source they use regularly. If you are familiar with it, try and ensure that they become fully aware of all its key features and how best to construct a search strategy when using it. Once a current question of interest to them becomes obvious, use it to explore other relevant information resources that you wish to bring to that individual's attention. Try to score one information hit during the session so that they go away from the teaching session feeling positive about the experience.

Other individuals may be shy and timid. Try to be relaxed and encouraging as you work through the tuition.

- Give them opportunities to ask questions and go over aspects of the topic as required.

- Be prepared to explain key points in a number of ways until they feel sure that they understand.

- Allow them to undertake searching of various information sources as part of the teaching and learning process to build their confidence.

- Never appear irritated.

It may have been difficult for people to come forward and ask for help and tuition and they may benefit from further teaching sessions and future refresher sessions. Always try to make the information skills training experience enjoyable and positive.

The independent end-user

Some library users have an independent streak that gives them the confidence to search for information unaided. Often this confidence is misplaced. They will embark on a computer search of a database or start searching the Internet, usually in great haste and then panic when they cannot remember what to do next or when the results they get are puzzling. You will be called upon (quite literally sometimes from an adjoining room) for help. You are faced with delivering one-to-one tuition to someone who does not think they need it. Impatiently they wait for you to 'sort out' their problem without giving you much information about what it is they are looking for. As you try to wrestle the search back and explain how to build up a search strategy, this type of end-user may try and anticipate what you are about to say and happily start clicking ahead of your explanation and loose the point of your help and part of their search, thus failing to secure some useful search results. This means that you have to retrieve the situation once again! These end-users rarely regard the help you give as tuition and fail to absorb the information you try to convey. This means that they rely on your help many times over.

You may not have any end-users like this or perhaps only one or two. Get to know them, assess their searching skills and tailor your interventions to meet their needs – this is a subtle form of one-to-one tuition. Try and improve their searching skills by slowing them down, if possible, and make the searching steps that are missing from their knowledge more interesting to them. If you can demonstrate that better searching equals better results and hold their attention a little more on each occasion they ask for help, you may harness their enthusiasm and translate it into true confidence when searching. These end-users are challenging but once they have appreciated what you can offer, they may well become real advocates of the library and information service.

If you have an increasing number of confident end-users who happily undertake their own searching with apparent success, regard this as a testament to your training initiatives. Observe your end-users as they search for information and be mindful of moments of uncertainty. Tactfully intervene if the opportunity arises to guide and help them with their searching. Point out the availability of training notes in connection with a particular database or useful online help.

All such interactions will build a good working relationship between you and your end-users.

External training situations

You may be asked to contribute to a library or information element of an external event. Organisers of a workshop or conference may wish to highlight library and information services within your organisation or institution. This may take the form of manning an information stand. This will give you an opportunity to display all the key information about your service and perhaps give a demonstration of important databases and information resources. The time you have to interact with delegates may be brief and in short bursts at refreshment break times. It will not be possible to embark upon any in-depth training but use all your experience to convey a few essential facts and searching tips to those people who express an interest in your stand. Make clear to them any opportunities to follow up with more detailed help and how to contact you to arrange such help. Often little gifts are provided as part of the conference pack – pens, bookmarks or notepads. Ask if one of these can be personalised with library information.

Alternatively, you may be asked to make a poster presentation at a conference or seminar. The topic will be of your choosing and drafting. Reflect all the key ideas you wish to communicate as you prepare the poster stand. Use the interaction with delegates showing an interest in your stand to enhance their understanding of the service or database or information resource you are highlighting. This is another form of one-to-one tuition and help. It also promotes your service.

You may be asked to be available at a conference or similar event to offer searching skills assistance, in dedicated time slots, as part of the overall programme. This indicates that skilled searching for information is regarded as an important element in the work of those attending the conference. The training that you deliver in these circumstances will be of great value but will often take place in far from ideal conditions. Often computers will be set up in a crowded room as a temporary arrangement with short-term subscription agreements to cover the use of various databases. Such impermanent arrangements can give rise to technical faults and some faltering of the data sets available. Always check out what printing or downloading facilities are available and try to restrain delegates from lengthy printouts that may clog up the computer network. The Internet connections may be unreliable.

Ideally you should be able to have access to the training room with time to check out the computer settings. Often this is not possible because delegates have been assigned project work to carry out during the conference and need to make use of the computers at various times during the day. So be prepared to take a seat at a computer at about the same time as the delegate or delegates you are about to help also sit down. The room may be quite noisy and everyone may find it difficult to concentrate. Quite frequently at national or international conferences there will be several foreign delegates and you will face language barriers to your training efforts. Always there will be time constraints within the conference programme. However, without exception the delegates will be committed to learning.

Harness all the skills you have developed with regard to your in-house training sessions and training programme. Have a detailed mental checklist of all the important issues that delegates, who may be novice searchers, should be made aware of as they look at some familiar and some new information sources. Try to establish a rapport with the person you are helping and give them sufficient time to explore for themselves some of the databases and other resources you wish them to become familiar with. Demonstrate as you explain some key points – this visual one-to-one help can be a valuable aid to information absorption. You will probably not meet the person you are helping again, unless there are open informal time slots at the end of each day for delegates to use the computers with library and information professionals on hand to give help.

The impact of your training slot may influence the delegate's view of the benefit of searching skills. Any training you can give must be short and to the point. Draw on all your experience of reacting to the needs of an individual library user, pull together all the knowledge you have about particular data sources and try to merge these into a relaxed but keenly paced mini training package. It will be exhausting but very interesting.

Communication

Think carefully at all times before you speak. Ensure that the language you use is easy to understand. Avoid jargon. Be aware of the specialist terms it may be necessary to use and always have a simple explanation available to clarify any queries. Encourage questions to be asked. Always be willing to answer these questions as fully as possible. Try not to rush through any explanation or presentation. Give your end-users time to absorb new facts and information. Allow them to reflect on what has been said or demonstrated. Try to avoid confusion or presenting information in a way that can be misinterpreted. Your message must be clear.

Telephone help

As people increasingly search for information at their desk, with access to networked information and the Internet, you may be asked for advice and help over the telephone.

It is not easy to become an instant telephone advisor, lacking the advantage of visual aids and eye contact with the enquirer. Envisage every step of a search sequence or task and describe it in as much detail as possible, pausing to assess whether or not your enquirer has understood and is ready for the next step. All the detailed training notes you have prepared will help you in this task.

In many organisations or associations that are spread over a wide area, contact with library and information staff may nearly always be by telephone or post. Staff working in such situations will need to develop appropriate skills to deliver skills training sessions from a central point.

Training notes will require conversion into alternative formats. This could be a networked e-learning package covering all the topics you would in other circumstances offer as a one-to-one or group training experience. It might be feasible to create a skills training CD that could be mailed to individuals within a diverse organisational structure. Remote one-to-one tuition, as an outreach activity, could be offered after initial end-user use of the training materials you have sent out or networked to them. This additional personal help will consolidate their learning experience.

The group training experience

Chapter contents

This chapter provides coverage of:

- learning styles;
- barriers to learning;
- basic skills;
- training sessions;
- single repeated training sessions;
- multi-sessional training;
- workshop planning;
- training evaluation;
- future planning.

Introduction

You may have the opportunity and time to be able to offer a variety of skills training sessions designed for specific staff groups and dedicated to specific ability groups. However, more usually you will be faced with mixed ability groups.

Learning styles

People learn in different ways. It is important to be aware of the nature of learning and try to respond to the differing demands of your group. Some group members could by their behaviour cause you to repeat several stages of your programme. They may linger in their thoughts and not follow what you are saying or presenting and then interrupt to ask a question about something you have already covered. Others, on the other hand, will, through their enthusiasm, anticipate the topics to be covered and ask questions about them out of sequence. Beware of jumping ahead yourself and so confusing the rest of the group! Indicate that this aspect or issue will be dealt with later in the session – encourage them to keep listening and to pay attention!

Learner types

- *Active* – these people like to be involved and contribute to the proceedings. They do not mind putting their ideas forward and they enjoy what they are doing.

- *Passive or reflective* – these people prefer to sit and listen; they do not like to be the centre of attention. They are happier observing and thinking about the ideas being put forward and then reflecting on them in their own time.

- *Theoretical* – these people like to adopt a methodical step-by-step approach to learning and to think things through in an analytical way.

- *Practical* – these people enjoy intervening and getting into hands-on sessions. They like practical solutions and enjoy trying out new ideas.

When working with individuals try to identify their preferred learning style and respond accordingly. In the group situation, ensure that you use a variety of teaching methods in the delivery of your skills training sessions. Employ visual aids and demonstrations, group discussions, participative activities and hands-on experience where possible.

It is recognised that many people will only take away a limited amount of information from any one skills training session. Opportunities for follow-on and follow-up training should be provided. Many people are very busy and feel unable to attend more than one or two skills training sessions. For these people it is useful to have handouts and notes that they can take away for reference and as a reminder of the topics they have covered. Always encourage your end-users to contact you after skills training sessions for further advice and help.

If you know that the group you are training may not be able to repeat or follow-up the training, it may be necessary to cover a wide range of information bordering on 'information overload'. This will at least make your end-users aware of the comprehensive nature of the information sources you are discussing and demonstrating. In the future, when they really need to use one of those sources for themselves in some detail, they may be prompted to ask for further help to explore the information source more carefully.

You can adopt a modular approach to the skills training sessions. Plan out an introductory, intermediate and advanced programme designed to have clear-cut parameters for each element. This may allow you to dedicate time to cover in detail specific aspects of the skills training, database searching or Internet resource in stages. This can work. However, not every end-user can commit to attending several training sessions and may drop out along the way. Some people will go away quite happily after an initial training session and feel confident about making a start on searching out information for themselves. This is good but unless they are aware of what further things they could do to improve their searching techniques or that there is a greater variety of information resources out there, they may remain at an early learning stage permanently. You will have to judge for yourself the most suitable approach to the planning and content of your skills training programmes.

Barriers to learning

Hopefully everyone attending a skills training session wants to attend and wants to learn. A key motivator is often a desire to solve a current work problem or question. However, some staff may have been told to attend one of your sessions or a workshop and are reluctant learners who may disrupt the sessions by trying to demonstrate that they do not find them helpful. They flatten the enthusiasm of others taking part. Try and identify anyone like this early in the session and seek to involve him or her in some way so that they can begin to participate. If you can use a topic that they have expressed an interest in to demonstrate a related information source, they may start to appreciate the relevance of the exercise.

Are the chairs comfortable? This can be a major problem. Is the training room too hot and stuffy or too cold? The physical environment is important to the learning process. Is the training room well lit? It is important for participants to be able to see their computer screens comfortably. Is the timing of the training sessions convenient to those wishing to attend? If someone is trying to fit too much into the working day or attend training between other commitments, they may loose concentration and start clock watching. Often, it may only be possible to arrange training sessions in lunchtime slots. This means that people will often arrive late with a sandwich in their hand or their head full of their previous work and take time to adjust to the training activity. It also means that you are faced with restarting the session several times, which is unfair on those participants who have managed to arrive on time.

Think about these issues and work out a strategy to deal with them. After one restart, it may be better to continue with the programme and attempt to talk to the late comers at the end of the session and quickly fill in some key issues they may have missed or explain carefully the handouts or notes and how best they can use them. You can also suggest that they might like to attend a future training session to revise the points that they might not have fully understood.

Basic skills

Before detailed subject-specific information skills training work can begin, it is important to assess the computer skills of your end-users. Many of the information resources to be demonstrated will require basic computer literacy skills. If an organisation has a computer network, it is easy to assume that individual employees and library users will possess the necessary keyboard skills and knowledge of software applications. It is time-consuming and disruptive to group work to have to stop and explain quite simple procedures. It can be helpful to prepare a short, basic computer competency presentation so that participants will be better able to employ word processing skills that will feature in all their computer activity. You may be faced with devising this training yourself but hopefully you can engage support from the IT or training departments within your organisation. If it is considered that presentational skills and an ability to project ideas and information will play an important role in their work, participants may benefit from a dedicated session on this topic or perhaps some pre-training on this could be arranged within your organisation.

If you do not address these issues, you may find yourself constantly interrupted with queries about 'how to do it' rather than 'how to find it'. Time taken to help with these enquiries can slow down the progress of the group as a whole and cause some participants to become frustrated and bored.

Training sessions

There is common ground in the preparation for all skills training sessions. It is important to state clearly the aims and objectives of any training session. Make it clear if any prerequisite skills are needed. Outline the specific topics to be taught in the session and list the expected outcomes to meet these objectives. Below are some examples.

1. *By the end of the session/course the participants should be able to:*

    – search effectively for (subject-specific) information on the Internet;

    – evaluate the quality of websites;

    – understand the nature and scope of Internet resources for (a specific subject);

- use (a named Internet resource) to answer a variety of set questions.

2. *By the end of the session/course the participants should be able to:*

- develop a detailed search plan or strategy for an advanced level search;

- select the best subject headings from the database thesaurus for each separate concept, exploding and focusing headings and including subheadings where relevant;

- carry out keyword searches where necessary to supplement subject heading searches;

- search individual fields to retrieve specific information;

- use the range of Boolean operators to combine sets;

- apply limits to refine and narrow the search;

- assess and evaluate the relevance and quality of the results found;

- where facilities exist, save search strategies on a temporary or permanent basis.

Such outcomes can be measured by testing within the skills training session itself or self-assessment by participants at the end.

As the trainer your prime task is to enable the group you are working with to acquire a certain level or amount of skill or understanding. Structure your training sessions with this aim in mind. Prepare too much material at first. This will help you sift through everything that you have assembled and really decide what the key components are that should be included in the training session(s). Have 'extra' examples or exercises for hands-on work – you may have eager, fast-working participants. Be prepared to take critical comments and learn from them.

Much of the time and effort you are able to devote to skills training will depend on the nature of your working environment and job description. You may not have previous experience of offering information skills training to end-users. You may be confident in responding to informal requests for help and instruction but unsure about expanding your training to more formal group work. Or you may have experience of such training but are embarking on delivering it in new circumstances.

Single repeated training sessions

Identify all the specific databases or information sources you consider important enough to warrant offering training about to your end-users. Decide how many of these it is feasible to develop training notes and programmes for as part of an ongoing training programme. It is better to start with a smaller number of well thought-out training sessions that can be repeated over a period of time than be over-ambitious and try to cover everything on your list and get hopelessly overwhelmed. In this way you can test your training sessions and revise them in the light of experience and comments from end-users. Over time clearer organ-isational objectives may become apparent and these will influence your information skills training programme.

Multi-sessional training

You can develop a matrix of participant ability levels and degree of topic difficulty to plan a programme of training sessions over a period of time. This can become quite complex. Such a programme would probably only be tackled in situations where staffing levels and training facilities allowed such a longer-term strategy to evolve. The training notes and exercises produced for single repeated training sessions can feed into a multi-sessional programme.

Workshop planning

It may be possible to develop your single and multiple training session activity into a workshop programme. This will enable particular groups of staff to come together for a day or perhaps a week that is dedicated to progressing the information skills training agenda within your organisation. This involves a major commitment on the part of you as the trainer and of the participants who may have to take study leave. The expectations of participants will be high, and they may well be demanding.

It is vital to determine that you have the resources and support within your organisation to embark on planning and delivering a workshop programme. It will take a lot of hard work.

Questions to ask yourself

- Who could benefit from the workshop?
- How many people might attend? Will sufficient interest be shown in the venture?
- Can these people be best served in a workshop model, i.e. a concentrated learning opportunity over a short time-span, rather than attending other group training sessions over a period of time?

- Are suitable training rooms available in the library or within the organisation?

- Do you have access to a sufficient number of computers to facilitate good hands-on training? Do you have a computer-assisted learning suite within the library or your organisation? The best situation is for each participant to have access to a single computer for the duration of the workshop or alternatively for a computer to be shared between two participants. The danger is that one participant will dominate the searching process, so it may be useful to vary the sharing of computers. More than two people trying to share a computer causes problems of seeing the screen and having adequate input into the searching process. Some participants will then become disinterested and bored.

- Would external facilities need to be booked?

- Is funding available to cover the workshop costs within the library and information service budget, or can bids be made for specific one-off or ongoing funding to develop the programme?

- Do you have adequate staff time and commitment to undertake the task?

Only if you have positive answers to these questions should you embark on planning an information skills training workshop programme.

Timescale

It is not easy to put a workshop programme together quickly. All the practical issues will need to be resolved before you have a product to advertise or you invite participation.

Potential participants are usually busy people and need a good lead time into the date of the workshop to enable them to book out the time in their diaries and where necessary make arrangements for their work to be covered. Be realistic and only agree to proceed if you are confident that the workshop will work.

Applications for the workshop

Eligibility

The workshop format usually means that places are limited, unless you have staff resources to offer parallel sessions. State clearly who is eligible to attend the workshop. Do you intend to restrict the workshop to a specific staff group or ability level? If so, be strict in adhering to this policy. It will enable you to prepare very relevant training notes and exercises with that group in mind.

Number of places and waiting lists

Do not be tempted to allow 'just one more' into the group. The number you have decided upon will have depended on the accommodation and equipment available. Do not compromise. The overall training experience will be jeopardised for the participants if they are faced with sharing computers beyond the original workshop design or if they feel lost in a larger than expected working group.

Because people may have to drop out between booking a place and the workshop taking place, it is prudent to have a waiting list of those people wishing to attend your workshop. Ask people who fail to be allocated a place if they would like to be put on a waiting list for the workshop and if they would like to be notified of similar future workshops. Make the selection criteria for offering a late place clear to those on the waiting list. It may be a simple of case of taking the next name (first come first served basis) or priority may be given to a particular profession or grade.

Once the interest in the workshop has been established, the data from those on the waiting list can be used to decide about running the workshop again and how frequently. The data can be used to make a bid for further funding to facilitate running extra workshops or similar skills training activity. Equally, consider the range of people who have expressed an interest in attending the workshop and consider ways in which you might reach out to them through other training activities or by targeting their staff group more directly.

Pre-assessment process

Unless the workshop is intended to be very broad in its acceptance policy, it is useful to establish the competence levels of participants as part of the booking process. This will enable you to group participants together if several workshops are planned or plan graded exercise work based on ability. Utilise any 'training needs questionnaire' that you might have devised for your overall information skills training programme and adapt it to any specific needs of the planned workshop. Sometimes it may only be possible to ask about the existing skill levels of the group at the beginning of the workshop but participants may not be very willing to volunteer this information openly within the group.

It is probably better to keep the assessment form quite simple and cover the following points:

- Workshop title
- Name
- Job title/role/department/degree course etc.
- Place of work/organisation
- Access to a computer at work and/or home
- State confidence in:
  - using a mouse
  - using a keyboard
  - accessing the Internet
  - using web addresses
  - moving between web pages
  - saving websites for future reference
  - navigating the Windows operating system
  - using word processing software
  - using presentational software
- State knowledge of or familiarity with:
  - specific databases (list them)
  - different searching interfaces in relation to these databases
  - Boolean operators
  - limiting searches
  - Internet searching
  - search engines (list any that you particularly wish to know about)

You can very quickly summarise this data and have a clearer picture about the group of workshop participants and their needs. Many people will under or overestimate their abilities. In a longer workshop over a period of a few days it is easier to assess and revise the self-assessed competence levels.

Computers are such a part of our lives that it is easy to assume that everyone is computer literate. Some people are quite happy to book a holiday online but freeze at the prospect of using the Internet to search for work-related information. They may 'do' things on the Internet quite happily when they do not have to worry so much about quality issues. If they do not understand all the associated jargon they may not be able to follow instructions that are given during the workshop. Give assistance to these people without slowing down the workshop sessions and suggest that you might give them individual help during break times.

Workshop administration

Bookings

- Be organised and careful.
- Design clear booking forms.
- Circulate or post booking forms in good time.
- Keep accurate and tidy records of the names and contact details of everyone who has asked for a booking form.
- Keep an orderly file of all booking forms received and the replies given.
- Make an attendance list for the workshop.
- Create a 'waiting file'.

Confirmation and acceptance of places

It is important to confirm a place to a participant and request an acceptance of the place. Some people can be quite lax about following things through and what seemed a good idea to them at the point of making the application may at a later date seem less relevant. People are not always considerate about the possibility of spoiling a chance for someone else to attend.

Permission to attend

If a workshop is to take place outside a lunchtime slot and will require the participant to be absent from their usual place of work or study it is crucial that their line manager, departmental head or tutor has given permission for their attendance. Do not accept verbal assurances that this has been given to an individual. Devise the application form in such a way that a signature has to be obtained from an appropriate person giving permission for the applicant to attend – not just a 'squiggle' but a clear name, signature, position and contact telephone number.

Reminders

Send out reminders to participants or telephone them nearer to the workshop date. Do not allow the busy schedules of the participants to overshadow the workshop date in their consciousness and cause non-attendance or cancellation at a stage when those on the waiting list cannot take advantage of the vacant place.

Workshop obligations

Skills training workshops cost money, not just in terms of the facilities used and the time of the information professionals involved but all the associated costs related to those attending the workshop. Workshop participants must be committed to getting the most out of the skills training opportunity and it may be useful to devise exercise tasks to be completed at the end of the workshop to measure the acquired competencies of the participants. State clearly both the learning objectives of the workshop and any work commitments. Often, participants will groan at the prospect of having to undertake 'set' work exercises or in other ways demonstrate their abilities. However, once they embark on such work they usually find that they enjoy exploring their newfound skills and take pleasure in showing their achievements.

Workshop accommodation and equipment

Training rooms

Accommodation for the workshop is vital. If you have in-house training facilities you will be clear about the number of participants that can be accommodated and have information about the full range of equipment available. Prepare a checklist of essential and desirable facilities to have when using outside training venues. There may be a long waiting time for training dates, especially if you are looking to arrange a workshop lasting more than one day. It is not desirable to move a group between rooms and especially not between buildings during the workshop.

Speak to staff in the training department in your organisation if you have one and ask for their advice. They may have special arrangements or tariffs with organisations offering local training venues. Visit any outside venue yourself and assess things for yourself. Refresh your memory about any internal facilities you may be planning to use. Only go ahead when you are sure everything will work for the programme you are planning.

Computers and IT support during the workshop

Most information skills training workshops will involve the use of computers. It is therefore vital that you have an adequate number of machines available for use throughout the workshop.

- Do the computers come with the training room?
- Do you have access to a mobile training laboratory?
- What arrangements have to be made to make use of such equipment?

Do not leave anything to chance.

- Double-check every aspect of the equipment.
- What help can you call on during the workshop in the event of computer failure or Internet connection failure? Is a computer technician on call to resolve problems?
- Do you have any equipment in reserve?
- Can you offer printing or downloading facilities? Make details of any of these services clear to the participants.
- What are your own computer troubleshooting abilities? Be honest.

Take care that you do not shake the confidence of the workshop participants by showing incompetence yourself in using the computer equipment. Equipment out of action also means that the workshop programme will slip and changes or curtailments will be forced upon the group.

Workshop security and emergencies

Personal security

Ensure that all participants are aware of the arrival and check-in procedures at the building where the workshop is being held. Staff should wear their identity badges. Encourage people to be vigilant about their personal belongings and arrange for the training room to be locked when not in use. Be aware of security procedures and security staff within your organisation and take the necessary action if an item is stolen.

Security of equipment

Ensure that all the equipment being used is accounted for at the beginning and end of each session. If items of equipment are on loan from other departments within your organisation, make sure that you have written authority for their use and that any related insurance matters are clarified. When using external facilities ensure that any contract you sign covers all these issues to your satisfaction. Check your liability.

Emergencies

Make clear to all workshop participants the procedures in the event of a fire. Demonstrate exits and assembly points. Indicate the location of toilets, first aid and other facilities.

Housekeeping arrangements

You must make it clear whether or not refreshments are included in the workshop event. It is usual to offer coffee and tea breaks, perhaps with biscuits. Once a group of participants have assembled, it is a good idea to keep them together for the duration of the workshop to facilitate a sharing of experience and ideas. It is therefore better to budget for full catering. Usually a sandwich or snack lunch will suffice. Give menu choices to allow for special dietary requirements such as vegetarian or diabetic options.

If canteen or restaurant facilities are immediately available try and arrange a group table for lunch with vouchers given to cover the cost. Alternatively make it clear that lunch is not included and indicate the likely cost of a meal in the facilities on site. Often refreshments are served in the training room itself or an adjoining room.

Decide on realistic break times. Allow sufficient time for participants to go to the cloakrooms or have a meal at the restaurant, and perhaps offer the opportunity to take a brief break outside for fresh air.

Workshop folder

To reflect the effort you put into the planning and arrangements for the workshop it is fitting that a 'Workshop

Folder' be produced containing a fully detailed programme, a list of participants and all core workshop training notes. Exercise sheets can be issued separately. This allows for last-minute updated changes to reflect the group composition or to highlight recent information resources. The folder can also contain some background information of interest to the participants that will not feature as part of a specific training session. For example, you could include some computer literacy notes if you are unable to devote time to these topics but it is clear from pre-assessment findings that some or all of the participants would benefit from such help.

Guidance on preparing training notes and exercise sheets can be found in Chapter 5.

Workshop evaluation

Evaluation forms

Evaluation forms can be useful. They can inform future planning. People are not always interested in filling them in at the end of a training session and promise to send them back later. Often they fail do this. Try to devise a simple form that does not seem too daunting and allow time at the end of the workshop to fill them in before the participants leave. If the workshop is of a longer duration it can be helpful to build in a 'talk-back' session that allows everyone to contribute their ideas about the usefulness to them of the workshop and suggest ideas for future training requirements.

Seek out examples of evaluation forms in relation to training. Discuss with colleagues the issues to identify for comment and draft a form based on these ideas. You can ask participants to comment on each training session and whether it met their needs and expectations, and to comment on the quality of the trainer(s) and the range and quality of the training materials. You can also ask for opinions about the training venue, facilities and refreshments. Select a scale, perhaps from 0 to 4, and indicate the value to each point on the scale – poor, good, very good, excellent – as appropriate.

A separate evaluation measurement can relate to their increased skills levels. You can repeat a version of the pre-assessment form to try and compare their self-assessed outcomes. This before and after snapshot can show the perceived progress of the participants and can be considered in conjunction with an analysis of the marking of any tasks you may have set the group. All this data will aid an assessment of the workshop programme.

Own assessment, evaluation and review

Try and annotate each training session with a checklist of objectives and desired outcomes and find time to record information against each session for review at the end of the workshop. It is easy to think that you will remember this or that later on but often the moment and valuable details are lost.

If you are offering training about a variety of different databases it can be helpful to ask the participants a short list of questions at the end of each session (or give them a brief question sheet to complete at the end of each session – this is not as problematic as it may appear). This 'on-the-spot' assessment of their understanding can help you identify issues that are not being fully understood by the group or individuals. You can use this information to devise a revision session towards the end of the workshop to cover and explain topics again, perhaps using different examples, so that everyone has an opportunity to fully grasp the topics under discussion. It also gives you an opportunity to seek out individuals who need help if they have put their name on the question sheets or raised a problem in discussion. A short spell of individual tuition can work wonders.

Why evaluate your training?

- To help you decide if the training and format made a difference – did participants go away having learned what you intended them to learn?
- To show whether or not the range of resources available to your end-users is known about.
- To demonstrate the need for further funding or support.
- To help redesign coursework and training materials in the light of comments and observations.
- To assess the place of information skills training within the overall service delivery of the library and information service.

Hopefully workshop participants will enjoy the information skills training sessions and go away better prepared to undertake information seeking and searching for themselves and with an understanding of the range of specialist resources available to them. They may then want to have further training opportunities offered or repeat workshops may be required for additional staff groups and to help those people on the waiting list.

Once the first workshop is over, you will have the experience to take training issues forward. You will have an informed view about the skill levels of your end-users and how to identify their training needs. The training notes and exercises can be used again, subject to revision and up-to-date examples being included. The full workshop programme can be broken down into segments and the preparation you have done put to good use in shorter skills training sessions for smaller groups.

A successful workshop can be an enriching experience for you as the information skills trainer but be prepared for adverse comments. Learn from what is said within the workshop and try to see the learning experience from the view of participants.

Electronic resources and the computer gateway

Chapter contents

This chapter provides coverage of:

- the computer gateway;
- Internet service providers;
- browsers;
- the World Wide Web;
- search engines and directories;
- URLs;
- quality information gateways and portals;
- subject-specific resources;
- action on retrieval;
- general searching tips.

Introduction

More and more people expect to search for information on the Internet. This is the way forward. They may happily look for information or services in their personal lives but are unsure about applying these skills in the work environment. They may use library-based resources with confidence but feel uncertain about obtaining quality material on the Internet working alone at their desk. Desktop access to information, removed from the library as a physical entity, means that library and information professionals must be vigilant about being involved in widening information horizons for their end-users. They must network resources to their end-users across their organisations.

Try to be associated with any initiatives involving web page design or content for your organisation and ensure that a library presence is made. Demonstrate all the resources that are funded by the library service, show how they can be used and searched effectively and market skills training opportunities via the network links.

In circumstances where computer networking is not up and running within your organisation, try networking in other ways. Reach out to staff or students in different departments or sectors using mail shots and personal visits to introduce library users and potential users to the range of services and resources you have available. End-users may still benefit from help and advice about Internet searching because they often use their home computers to complement their workplace resources. Encourage them to use e-mail and bulletin board communication.

It can be useful to prepare some simple notes about the Internet giving a reminder or explanation about some of the jargon involved. This material can be used to set the scene at the beginning of any general Internet skills training you give. For those end-users who have limited computer skills and knowledge this will remove some of the myths surrounding the World Wide Web. Some suggested topics to cover in your notes are given below.

Internet service providers

Many end-users will be familiar with using their organisational network facilities where everything appears seamless. It can be useful to remind them of what is required when setting up an Internet connection at home. They will need an Internet service provider (ISP) to give access to the Internet, for example BT (British Telecom) or AOL (America On Line). Standalone PCs require a modem to dial up an Internet provider. Advise end-users to check that calls are being offered at a local rate for home use. There are a variety of charges and subscription rates plus broadband options.

Browsers

Browsers are software programs that allow you to read and see information on the World Wide Web (www). Key browsers are Microsoft Internet Explorer (*http://www.microsoft.com*) and Netscape Navigator (*http://www.netscape.com*).

Many websites have a UK home page with .co.uk instead of .com. Try this to limit your search or look for other ways of excluding non-national material if required.

What is the World Wide Web (www)?

The Internet is a global network of computers connected electronically by telephone lines, fibre-optic cables and other links. This allows the sharing and exchange of information 24 hours a day. It links documents together so that, by using the computer mouse, you can jump from document to document, even if the documents are on different computers around the world. These highlighted links, and images, are called hypertext links. Double click on the hypertext to activate the link. Clicking from one document to another and so on gave rise to the term 'surfing' the Net.

What is on the Internet?

Something can be found on almost any topic – travel, employment, law, government statistics, cooking, health, etc. All kinds of people and organisations put information on the Web. The skill is being discerning about the quality and reliability of the information retrieved.

Search engines and directories

Search engines and directories allow general searching across the Internet. They use automated specialist searching software often called spiders or mega crawlers to search for information based on their own criteria to create indexes of the web. You then search the databases that are created from this process. The extent to which each page is indexed and to what level the information is reviewed varies between the different search engines. Relevancy of the items found is ranked according to their own algorithms.

There is usually a search box where you type in a key word or phrase. Search engines tend to return an inordinate number of hits but they usually offer an 'advanced' or 'refined' search feature that will allow you to reduce the number of items to scan through (see the online help for how to apply these techniques). Results are usually presented in relevance order.

It is essential to scan the list of hits and try to evaluate the nature of the resources. Very limited annotations or subject organisation of the items are given. However, search engines do offer extensive coverage of the Internet and are updated regularly.

What are you searching?

Much of the material is ephemeral in nature and lacks peer reviewing or the editorial and refereeing process. Self-publicity is easy. Two-thirds of Internet information is in database format, including electronic journals, and is invisible to search engines.

Examples of popular search engines are:

- *Google (http://www.google.com)*. Google is a very popular search engine providing access to more than 4 billion web pages. It uses sophisticated text-matching techniques to find web pages that are important and relevant to your search. It is very comprehensive with great relevancy.

- *Alta Vista (http://www.altavista.com)*. Altavista is a leading provider of search services and technology. Among its many features it has a 'translate' option allowing translation into nine languages. The results come from Yahoo and tabs above each search box let you go beyond the web search to find images, MP3/audio, video, human category listings and news results.

- *HotBot (http://www.hotbot.co.uk/)*. Hotbot has powerful features. It provides easy access to the web's three major crawler-based search engines: Yahoo, Google and Teoma. Unlike a meta-search engine (see below) it cannot blend the results together but it is a fast, easy way to get different web results in one place.

Subject indexes are useful if you want to browse and see what is available on a particular subject, rather like browsing along a shelf of books or looking in a library card catalogue. They offer hierarchical listings of Internet resources. Yahoo (*http://www.yahoo.com*) is one of the best known and is the oldest 'directory'. It has websites arranged by subject, with major subject categories and subcategories. Increasingly the distinction between search engines and search directories is not made and the term search engine is applied.

Meta-search engines

Meta-search engines are designed to allow simultaneous access to a number search engines. This has the advantage of knowing that you will have covered a variety of approaches to the subject but the process may be slow. Two examples are: Search.com (*http://search.com*) (this searches Google, Ask Jeeves, LookSmart and dozens of other leading search engines) and WebCrawler (*http://webcrawler.com*) (this searches Google, Yahoo, Ask Jeeves, LookSmart, Overture and Find What).

Web addresses

If you have a web address (or uniform resource locator (URL)) for a site you wish to visit then type this in at the address prompt line at the top of the page and hit the return button. The address usually begins *http://www*. 'Http' stands for hypertext transfer protocol, which is the standard language that World Wide Web clients and servers use to communicate. This will then connect you to that site – a progress bar along the bottom of the computer screen shows you how quickly the connection is being made. Graphics on a page or congestion at the service provider's server can cause delays.

You will see the address of any web page you are at displayed in the address line. Use this address information to help evaluate the reliability of a site/web page. Check to see if an acknowledged organisation, association, society, university or government department is depicted in the address. Check the domain name of the website: ac = educational establishment (edu in America or Australia); gov = government sites; org = non-profit organisations and co/com = commercial companies (UK and US equivalents).

Look at the URL – does it contain an organisation's name that you recognise? Try deleting part of the address line until you reach the stem that would take you to the home page of that organisation. The URL is rather like a filing cabinet and each forward slash / takes you into a more detailed file. If you use an URL that does not work or a page cannot be displayed then back track through the URL until you reach the home page element and start with a fresh search of that website to locate information. It may be that the particular page relating to the URL you are trying to use has now been withdrawn or edited in someway and given a new URL, i.e. it has been filed in a different place.

An example of a web address is: *http://* (the protocol) *www.now.ac.uk/* (the domain name) *publications/* (the path) *report.htm* (the filename). An Internet address is composed of some or all of these parts. Check the domain to see if the author, organisation or institution is recognisable.

Remember that ISPs host web pages, i.e. are technically the publisher/author, but they will not have any knowledge of the content.

Quality information gateways or portals

These have tailored subject content created by people with specialist subject knowledge. They may offer subject-specific indexing and classification. Coverage is highly selective on the basis of predetermined and stated criteria. Every website included in a gateway should have been carefully evaluated for quality and relevance. This can reassure the searcher that they will be finding quality material and removes from them the task of filtering the results. The number of hits will be much less than when using a search engine, reflecting the detailed human input.

Websites to look at include the following:

- *BUBL* (*http://bubl.ac.uk/*). This information gateway for higher education and research offers free user-friendly access to selected Internet resources covering all subject areas, with a special focus on library and information science.

- *HERO* (*http://www.hero.ac.uk/uk/home/index.cfm*). HERO (Higher Education and Research Opportunities in the UK) is the official gateway to universities, colleges and research organisations in the United Kingdom.

- *OMNI* (*http://www.omni.ac.uk/*). OMNI (Organising Medical Networked Information) offers free access to a searchable catalogue of hand-selected and evaluated, quality Internet resources in health and medicine. New resources are added to the database on a weekly basis.

- *SOSIG* (*http://www.sosig.ac.uk*). SOSIG (the Social Science Information Gateway) aims to provide a trusted source of selected, high-quality Internet information for researchers and practitioners in the social sciences, business and law. It is part of the UK Resource Discovery Network.

Explore for yourself a selection of search engines. Run the same search on each of them and evaluate their speed and relevancy for producing satisfactory results. It can be an enlightening exercise to ask a group of end-users at a training session to look at a variety of topics across several search engines and ask for their assessment of each of them. A good discussion often results.

Look on the Internet for detailed information about a range of search engines and directories. Keep up to date with developments and pass on information about changes to your end-users. If you produce a library newsletter or bulletin, include a regular Internet or IT news item.

Two useful websites to explore for information are: *http://www.searchenginewatch.com* and *http://www.philb.com/*.

Subject-specific electronic resources

Most databases include journal articles and perhaps conference proceedings or reports. Your end-users may be familiar with searching for this type of resource in your library or via your network. Introduce your end-users to new resources. Explore a variety of topics, especially those related to the subject speciality of your library service, and evaluate the websites you find. This will enable you to draw up a list of suggested or recommended websites for your end-users to try for themselves where a great variety of different resources and documents can be found. Here are some ideas:

- *Web of Knowledge (http://wok.mimas.ac.uk)*. This is a widely used multi-disciplinary dataset that covers articles from leading journals across a wide range of subjects. It comprises three large sub-files: the Science Citation Index (includes medicine and technology), the Social Sciences Citation Index and the Arts and Humanities Citation Index. These can be searched singly or together.

- *ZETOC (http://zetoc.mimas.ac.uk)*. Zetoc provides access to the British Library's Electronic Table of Contents of around 20,000 current journals and around 16,000 conference proceedings published per year. The database covers 1993 to date and is updated on a daily basis. It does not contain abstracts. Access is limited to UK higher education institutions and the NHS. A small number of other institutions are eligible to subscribe to Zetoc.

- *Books*. You can access some important library catalogues on the Web. The British Library (*http://www.bl.uk/*) is a huge resource, as is the catalogue of the US Library of Congress (*http://www.loc.gov/*).

- *Newspapers*. There are several useful gateways to newspaper information, for example: *http://www.thepaperboy.com/* for information on worldwide newspapers and *http://www.newsdirectory.com* which includes information about UK regional newspapers.

Action on retrieval

Many end-users are disorganised about how they keep information that they find as a result of an Internet search. It can be helpful to run through with them some of the key issues. Here are some pointers – you can adjust how you express the instructions.

General points

- Once in a website of interest that they might want to refer to again tell them to click on the *Favorites* button (in Microsoft Explorer) or *Bookmark* (in Netscape) on the top tool bar and select *Add*. Place the added item in the folder of their choice. Folders can be created in advance or at the time of adding (follow the on-screen instructions). When they click onto *Favorites* and then click onto a folder, a sub-list will appear of the various saved websites – click onto a selected one to connect. Review, edit and delete saved websites as appropriate at regular intervals to ensure that the listed websites are still active and that the overall list does not become too unwieldy. This may be more useful on a home computer. Shared computer resources in the library can produce a long list that has to be deleted and cleared from time to time.

- Advise them to become familiar with the process of saving and printing web material. Images may be embedded into a document and not appear when you print out the page after saving. They may need to be selected separately by clicking and highlighting and then saved independently. Many websites now have a printer-friendly version which can be printed mainly as text without the complexity of colour and extra features as seen on the screen.

- Remind them about *hypertext* links to other web pages. This can be a way of building up knowledge over a range of websites on a given subject.

- It is important for your end-users to be aware that web pages and Internet sites change frequently. What is current today may change tomorrow! Sometimes a forwarding web address is given for a short period but often it is a case of starting a fresh search to try and locate an up-to-date information source or to trace the original organisation that had produced that particular web page.

Tell your end-users that they can:

- Use the *Back* button to retrace their steps.

- Use the *Forward* button to reverse this.

- Use the *Stop* button to halt a search if it is taking too long.

- Click onto the *Home* button on the top line to return to the home page

- Use the *Refresh* button (*Reload* in Netscape Navigator) when they get a message saying that a web page cannot be displayed or when they want to make sure that they have the latest version of the web page.

- Use the *History* button to review the websites visited most recently. You can set the number of web pages to be kept in the History.

It is prudent to clear the *cache* at regular intervals. A copy of every website visited is stored on the computer hard drive for a quick response when the browser asks for that web page again. This cache is checked to see if a local copy exists;

if it does it will be seen very quickly. On some networks this information may be stored centrally.

To alter the History setting or to clear the cache go to *Tools* (in Microsoft) on the top bar and click on *Internet options* – this will then show a sub-screen in which both these dimensions can be edited.

Cookies need to be enabled to allow certain procedures to be carried out. Cookies are small pieces of information that a website puts onto a computer hard disk to allow information to flow between parts of the website. The mechanism allows your movements through the Web to be remembered (usually when you search the Web this does not happen). For example, if a database search is to be saved against a person's name for retrieval later the server where the information is to be stored must be able to identify the searcher again when prompted, or when compiling a shopping basket there will be various information-gathering screens to be coordinated.

Evaluating your results

As with any literature searching or information retrieval, it is important to evaluate the results with care. In judging the quality of a web page ask yourself the following questions:

- Who is the author? Is it an individual, a commercial concern, a pressure group or a charity? Can you verify the contact details?

- What authority does the information have? Is it clear that the author is qualified to write the document? Check the website domain.

- Is the basis of the information clear? Is it designed to inform or amuse or advertise? Check for objectivity or bias.

- Is the web page or document up to date? When was the website last updated and are links current?

For further information about how to go about evaluating websites look at the following:

- the Virtual Training Suite: *http://www.vts.rdn.ac.uk/* – look at the *Internet for Reference* section, Instructor Tutorial under the review section;

- the Internet Detective: *http://www.sosig.ac.uk/desire/ internet-detective.html*.

TIPS: Thoughts to Inform People on Searching – a summary

Before you start a search on the Internet

- Specify your information needs.

- Define your search and frame the question to be answered – this may have to be simpler than when you are searching a structured and fully indexed database.

- Break the subject or topic down into component parts.

- Think about all the key concepts or words associated with the question.

- Make a note of both British and American spelling if relevant to the subject.

- Try using quotation marks to indicate a phrase so that the search identifies more accurately what you are looking for. However, not all electronic resources support phrase searching.

- Some search engines recognise the + sign and – sign to indicate inclusion or exclusion of a word. Leave a space before entering the plus or minus symbols. This is helpful when a word that is essential to your search may be excluded under the 'automatic exclusion of common words' employed by most search engines, e.g. where.

- Usually, if more than one word is entered, the searching software will return web pages that include all the search terms. Check online guidance about any particular search engine.

- Check the Help screen for specific information on such things as the use of truncation – usually the symbol is * or $.

- Think about limiting the search (e.g. date or language) and check the options for doing this.

- When looking for an organisation be aware of its full title and its acronym.

Be organised!

- Surfing the Net can be fun but think in advance about how you want to organise useful websites.

- Be disciplined in examining carefully sources of information to ensure that they are reliable. DIY (do it yourself) evaluation is required.

- Limit searching sessions and be focused.

- Keep a careful note of every aspect of the searching process. This helps future searching to be more successful and assists in the evaluation of results.

Remember that there are other sources of useful information. Encourage your end-users to make use of any membership of professional associations and use their website or consult their colleagues and share experiences.

Once your end-users are confident about searching the Internet to seek information and are able to interpret and evaluate the results, they will increasingly use this avenue as a first resort. It is quick and it is easy if they have a computer on their desktop. You will need to plug into this activity and remind your end-users of other resources available to them that will complement their findings.

Internet search results can be overwhelming and end-users can be lulled into thinking that they have found 'everything'. Be alert to new websites or enhanced features introduced to frequently used websites. Target different staff groups with updates on subject-specific websites. Show them how to get the best out of them – this will require hard work on your part but it is important to continually demonstrate the specialist skills you have to offer.

Appendix 1
Sample information audit
questionnaire

On the following pages is an example of an information audit questionnaire drafted by voluntary library staff at St Helena's Hospice in Colchester, Essex. Help the Hospices Volunteer Project Grant, 'Information Audit of Users' Needs' 2004, funded the work.

St Helena Hospice Education Centre

Information Audit

Name   _____

Location   _____

Tel. no.   _____

E-mail address   _____

Job title   _____

Staff category   _____

Gender   _____

[Detachable Cover Sheet]

[Questionnaire]

1.   **Awareness of the library**

    1a. Were you aware that St Helena Hospice has a library?

         Yes   ☐   No   ☐

    1b. If No: Are you now likely to visit the library?

         Yes   ☐   No   ☐

    1c. If Yes to 1a: Have you visited the library?

         Yes   ☐   No   ☐

How did you first contact the library?

Personally	☐
Telephone	☐
Letter	☐
E-mail	☐

Other: please specify _____

1d. If No: Why have you not visited the library?

Is it because of the opening hours?

Yes ☐　　　　No ☐

Is it because of restriction of your own time?

Yes ☐　　　　No ☐

Are you aware that the library is available for everyone?

Yes ☐　　　　No ☐

Other: please specify _____

1e. Where do you get your information from?

Doctor	Friend	Local library	Internet	Other
☐	☐	☐	☐	☐

Other: please specify _____

1f. If Yes to 1c:　How frequently do you use or visit the library?

Daily (3+ times p.w.)	☐
Weekly	☐
Fortnightly	☐
Monthly	☐
Quarterly	☐
Occasionally (1–3 times p.a.)	☐
Never	☐

1g. Current opening hours vary Monday – Friday between 8.30 am and 4.30 pm.

What days of the week do you think the library should be open?

Monday ☐
Tuesday ☐
Wednesday ☐
Thursday ☐
Friday ☐
Saturday ☐
Sunday ☐

What hours do you think the Library should be open?

As it stands ☐
Monday From _____ To _____
Tuesday From _____ To _____
Wednesday From _____ To _____
Thursday From _____ To _____
Friday From _____ To _____
Saturday From _____ To _____
Sunday From _____ To _____

If these hours are not feasible would you like a late evening?

Yes ☐   No ☐

If Yes: Which day of the week would most suit you?

Monday ☐
Tuesday ☐
Wednesday ☐
Thursday ☐
Friday ☐
Saturday ☐
Sunday ☐

1h. On your first visit to the library were you given an induction to the services?

Yes ☐   No ☐   Don't know ☐   N/A ☐

1i. Were you given a leaflet about the library?

Yes ☐   No ☐   Don't know ☐   N/A ☐

1k. Were the following services explained to you?

	Yes	No	Don't know	N/A
Library catalogue	☐	☐	☐	☐
Library classification system	☐	☐	☐	☐
Layout of the library	☐	☐	☐	☐
Procedures	☐	☐	☐	☐
Book loans	☐	☐	☐	☐
Leaflets	☐	☐	☐	☐
Availability of Athens password	☐	☐	☐	☐
Databases	☐	☐	☐	☐

2. Staffing

2a. How helpful have you found the library staff?

Not helpful	Sometimes helpful	Helpful	Very helpful
☐	☐	☐	☐

2b. Where staff have helped you, how satisfied were you with the result?

Not satisfied	Sometimes satisfied	Satisfied	Very satisfied
☐	☐	☐	☐

3. Services

3a. Please indicate your awareness and use of the following services provided by the library

	Aware	Use	Never
Book loans	☐	☐	☐
Reference collection	☐	☐	☐
Periodicals/journals	☐	☐	☐
Inter-library loans	☐	☐	☐
Photocopying	☐	☐	☐
Contents pages (from journals)	☐	☐	☐
Articles collection	☐	☐	☐
Video	☐	☐	☐
Study packs	☐	☐	☐
Teaching packs	☐	☐	☐
Archives	☐	☐	☐
Study area and reading room	☐	☐	☐
Databases	☐	☐	☐
Internet	☐	☐	☐
Library/Hospice web page	☐	☐	☐
Mediated searches	☐	☐	☐
Book sales	☐	☐	☐
Gift cards	☐	☐	☐

3b. Which of the library's resources do you use the most?

Books

Never	Sometimes	Frequently	Regularly	N/A
☐	☐	☐	☐	☐

Journals

Never	Sometimes	Frequently	Regularly	N/A
☐	☐	☐	☐	☐

Videos

Never	Sometimes	Frequently	Regularly	N/A
☐	☐	☐	☐	☐

4. Books

4a. Books are loaned for three weeks – would you say this was:

Too long ☐ Too short ☐ About right ☐

4b. Short-term book loans are for 2–7 days – would you say this was:

Too long ☐ Too short ☐ About right ☐

4c. How long/short do you think a short loan should be?

2 days	3 days	5 days	7 days	Longer
☐	☐	☐	☐	☐

4d. Are you aware that the library charges a 50p per day fine for overdue books?

Yes ☐ No ☐

4e. Were you aware that this fine has been set by APU (Anglia Polytechnic University)?

Yes ☐ No ☐

4f. How up to date do you find the book stock?

Poor	Good	Very good	Excellent
☐	☐	☐	☐

4g. How do you rate the coverage of the stock?

Poor	Good	Very good	Excellent
☐	☐	☐	☐

4h. Have you used the reference collection?

Yes ☐ No ☐

4i. How useful do you find the reference collection?

Poor	Good	Very good	Excellent
☐	☐	☐	☐

5. Journals

5a. At which sites do you access journals?

Hospice ☐
APU library ☐
Other university library ☐ Please specify _____
Other NHS library ☐ Please specify _____
Other location ☐ Please specify _____

5b. The library currently subscribes to 85 journals. Please indicate up to 5 journals that you consult in the library on a regular basis

1. _____
2. _____
3. _____
4. _____
5. _____

5c. Are you aware that the library has access to e-journals?

Yes ☐ No ☐

5d. Have you ever accessed any e-journals?

Yes ☐ No ☐

5e. How often do you access e-journals?

Never Sometimes Frequently Regularly
☐ ☐ ☐ ☐

5f. Would you be prepared to be involved in a Hospice journal survey?

Yes ☐ No ☐

6. **Videos**

   6a. The library holds a considerable number of videos. Have you watched any of them?

   Yes ☐   No ☐

   6b. Did you find them informative?

   Yes ☐   No ☐

   6c. How up to date do you find the videos?

Poor	Good	Very good	Excellent
☐	☐	☐	☐

   6d. How do you rate the coverage of the videos?

Poor	Good	Very good	Excellent
☐	☐	☐	☐

7. **Inter-library loans**

   The library currently charges 10p per page for journal items received as ILL.

   7a. How much would you be prepared to pay per page for an ILL article?

10p	15p	20p	25p	Other
☐	☐	☐	☐	☐

   Other: please specify _____

8. **Photocopying**

   8a. Are you aware that the library is limited, under the Copyright Act, as to the amount of material we are allowed to copy?

   Yes ☐   No ☐

8b. If No: would you like a leaflet?

    Yes   ☐   No   ☐

    Leaflet given   Yes   ☐

    Leaflet to be forwarded   Yes   ☐

The Library currently charges 6p per page for photocopying on a self-service basis or 10p per page if done by a member of staff.

8c. How much would you be prepared to pay per page for photocopying?

6p	10p	12p	15p	Other
☐	☐	☐	☐	☐

    Other: please specify _____

8d. How often do you use the photocopier?

Never	Sometimes	Frequently	Regularly
☐	☐	☐	☐

9. Contents pages

9a. Do you receive contents pages?

    Yes   ☐   No   ☐

9b. Do you read/study the contents pages?

Never	Sometimes	Frequently	Regularly
☐	☐	☐	☐

9c. Does this raise your awareness of issues in your field of interest/specialty?

Never	Sometimes	Frequently	Regularly
☐	☐	☐	☐

9d. Do the contents pages save you time?

Never	Sometimes	Frequently	Regularly
☐	☐	☐	☐

9e. Do you follow up – e.g. visit the library?

Never	Sometimes	Frequently	Regularly
☐	☐	☐	☐

9f. Do you have a current contents pages profile?

Yes ☐ No ☐

9g. Would you like your contents pages profile to be reviewed?

Yes ☐ No ☐

10. Articles collection

10a. Have you ever consulted the articles collection?

Yes ☐ No ☐

10b. How frequently do you use the articles collection?

Never	Sometimes	Frequently	Regularly
☐	☐	☐	☐

10c. How up to date do you find the articles collection?

Poor	Good	Very good	Excellent
☐	☐	☐	☐

10d. How do you rate the coverage of the articles collection?

Poor	Good	Very good	Excellent
☐	☐	☐	☐

11. Databases

11a. Were you aware that the library has access to the following databases?

	Yes	No
Medline	☐	☐
CINHAL	☐	☐
Cochrane	☐	☐
BNI	☐	☐
AMED	☐	☐
Encarta	☐	☐
Encyclopaedia Britannica	☐	☐

11b. Do you do your own literature searches?

Yes ☐　　　　　No ☐

11c. How easy do you find it to use databases?

Difficult	Not easy	Easy	Very easy
☐	☐	☐	☐

11d. Would you like to receive training on one of the following?

Literature searching	☐
Databases	☐
Internet	☐
Computer programs	☐
Other	☐

Other: please specify _____

11e. Has a member of staff done a literature search for you?

Yes ☐　　　　　No ☐

11f. If Yes: Did it answer your queries?

Yes ☐　　　　　No ☐

12. Internet

12a. Were you aware that the library is connected to the Internet?

Yes ☐   No ☐

12b. Did you know that the library has a website with Internet links?

Yes ☐   No ☐

12c. Have you visited it?

Yes ☐   No ☐

12d. If Yes: How helpful did you find it?

Not helpful	Sometimes helpful	Helpful	Very helpful
☐	☐	☐	☐

13. Subject coverage

13a. Do you think that there are any subject areas that are missing or inadequate in the library?

Please specify.

13b. How could the library best serve the hospice community, i.e. Tendering area, shops, warehouse, or anyone working away from the hospice?

Please specify.

14. Any other comments?

Note:

N/A = not answered or not applicable.

Appendix 2
Sample questionnaires from a distance learning project

The London Deanery, London Department of Postgraduate Medical and Dental Education, University of London, funded a Distance Learning Project in 2000. It aimed to help a group of 12 SpRs (specialist registrars) in psychiatry working as flexible trainees (part-time appointments) in the NHS. This group of staff were particularly disadvantaged in their access to information technology infrastructures and they lacked information-searching skills. A Project Officer visited the group in their homes over a 12-month period offering one-to-one tuition. Four workshop training sessions were also offered during the project.

This work was developed into a series of information skills workshops open to flexible trainees from all disciplines and overseas doctors. The medical background of the participants together with the database subject specialty and versions available at the time is reflected in the questions. General principles can be taken from the outlines.

Two examples of the questionnaires used are given below.

Distance Learning Project

The London Deanery and The London Library & Information Development Unit*

Skills Training Needs Assessment

Name:

Work location:

Professional responsibilities and interests:

Familiarity with IT and computers:

1. No computer use or experience	☐
2. Occasional use	☐
3. Regular use	☐
4. Work access to a PC	☐

Details from discussion:

Confidence with:

	Y	N
1. Windows operating system	☐	☐
2. MS Word	☐	☐
3. MS Excel	☐	☐
4. MS PowerPoint	☐	☐
5. Other word processing, spreadsheet or presentational software	☐	☐

Details from discussion:

Library use:

Previous information skills training:

Database use:

Which databases used?

1. Medline	☐ CD-ROM version	☐ Web version	☐
	Silver Platter		
	software	☐ OVID software	☐
2. The Cochrane			
Library	☐ CD-ROM	☐ Web version	☐
3. Cinahl	☐		
4. PsychLit or			
ClinPsych	☐		
5. Other			

Self-assessment on database searching skills:

1. A complete beginner	☐
2. Can do basic searches but would like to be able to refine searches	☐
3. Fairly experienced – which databases	☐
4. Experienced on some databases – specify	☐

Searching techniques:

	Y	N
1. Formulating a search strategy	☐	☐
2. Confidence about MeSH headings	☐	☐
3. Familiarity with Boolean operators	☐	☐
4. Use of truncation	☐	☐
5. Methods of limiting searches	☐	☐
6. Use of quality filters	☐	☐

Internet use:

	Y	N
1. Access to the Internet	☐	☐
2. E-mail communication	☐	☐
3. Bulletin board use	☐	☐
4. Leisure use	☐	☐
5. Sourcing biomedical information	☐	☐
6. PubMed use	☐	☐

Specific requests for help:

April, 2000

* The LLIDU closed in March 2003.

Note: This questionnaire was completed by the Project Officer during discussions with the project participants. Comments were recorded in the 'Details from discussion' spaces.

Distance Learning Project

The London Deanery and The London Library & Information Development Unit*

Evaluation Questionnaire

Name:

Date:

1. What prompted you to respond to the letter inviting you to participate in this project?

2. What were your expectations of the project?

3. What did you hope to achieve during the project?

4. List your three main achievements as a result of the project:

    a.

    b.

    c.

5. Can you now construct a search strategy that you are confident includes all aspects of your search topic?

    Yes ☐   No ☐

6. Have you used MeSH headings specifically in your searching?

   Yes ☐   No ☐

7. Do you understand the use of Boolean operators?

   a. Which operator would you use to focus
      a search?   ....
   b. Which operator will broaden a search? ....
   c. How can the 'NOT' operator help in a
      search strategy?

8. Have you used truncation in your searching?

   Yes ☐   No ☐

9. Do you understand how to limit your searches?

   Yes ☐   No ☐

10. Are you more familiar now with the use of quality filters compared to six months ago?

    Yes ☐   No ☐

11. Are you clear about the concepts of evidence-based healthcare?

    Yes ☐   No ☐

12. Which of the following databases have you used during the project?

    Medline   ☐
    The Cochrane Library ☐
    PubMed   ☐
    Other   ☐   Please specify

13. How often do you search the PubMed database?

    Occasionally   ☐
    Frequently   ☐

14. Are there any features in the PubMed database that you would like to have further help in using?

15. Which search engine do you find most user-friendly?

16. List (at least three) websites that you have found useful:

    a.
    b.
    c.

17. Which Internet service provider do you use?

18. Which e-mail system do you use?

19. Have you contacted fellow project participants via e-mail?

    Yes   ☐   No   ☐

20. Would you like to have had greater inter-group communication?

Yes ☐   No ☐

And why?

21. How frequently have you used a library service during the project?
    a. Occasionally   ☐
    b. Frequently   ☐
    c. In person   ☐
    d. By telephone/letter   ☐
    e. Never   ☐

22. Are you familiar now with basic functions in Windows software?

Yes ☐   No ☐

23. Can you now use the following software?
    a. Word   Yes ☐   No ☐
    b. PowerPoint   Yes ☐   No ☐

24. Could you carry out a CD-ROM Medline search using the following?

    a. Silver Platter WinSPIRS software   Yes ☐   No ☐

    b. OVID software   Yes ☐   No ☐

25. As the project ends, what assistance would you still welcome?

26. What are the positive aspects of the project that you think could be taken forward to help another group of flexible trainees?

27. Any other comments?

Thank you for your answers.

Project Officer

* The LLIDU closed in March 2003.

Index